PRODUCTIVITY
MEASUREMENT

Applied Social Research Methods Series
Volume 19

APPLIED SOCIAL RESEARCH
METHODS SERIES

Series Editor:
LEONARD BICKMAN, Peabody College, Vanderbilt University, Nashville
Series Associate Editor:
DEBRA J. ROG, Vanderbilt University, Washington, DC

PRODUCTIVITY MEASUREMENT

A Guide for Managers and Evaluators

Robert O. Brinkerhoff
Dennis E. Dressler

Applied Social Research Methods Series
Volume 19

SAGE PUBLICATIONS
The International Professional Publishers
Newbury Park   London   New Delhi

For information address:

SAGE Publications, Inc.
2111 West Hillcrest Drive
Newbury Park, California 91320

SAGE Publications Ltd.
28 Banner Street
London EC1Y 8QE
England

SAGE Publications India Pvt. Ltd.
M-32 Market
Greater Kailash I
New Delhi 110 048 India

Printed in the United States of America

Library of Congress Cataloging-in-Publication Data

Brinkerhoff, Robert O.
    Productivity measurement / Robert O. Brinkerhoff, Dennis E.
Dressler.
        p.   cm. — (Applied social research methods series ; v. 19)
    Includes bibliographical references.
    ISBN 0-8039-3151-4. — ISBN 0-8039-3152-2 (pbk.)
    1. Industrial productivity—Measurement.   I. Dressler, Dennis E.
II. Title. III. Series.
HD56.25.B75   1990
658.3'14—dc20   89-37840
                                                                                  CIP

SECOND PRINTING 1990

CONTENTS

FOREWORD

Companies and agencies all over the globe are facing increasing competition and a greater need than ever before to use resources more efficiently. Quality and productivity are widely recognized as the crucial factors that will enable organizations to survive in the hotly competitive world-wide marketplace. Quality circles, statistical process control, and productivity enhancement are but three of a variety of methods being touted for achieving competitive advantage. Common to virtually all of these increasingly popular methods is measurement: the ability to accurately diagnose current productivity problems, and the capacity to assess the results of productivity improvement solutions.

Historically, productivity measurement has been the province of economists and other experts. Yet the current need, in literally thousands of government agencies and businesses both large and small, is to implement simple and useful measurement procedures to empower managers to make badly needed improvements in productivity.

This book presents a thorough overview of the basics of productivity measurement, and at the same time provides a practical and straightforward guide to designing and using effective productivity measures. The authors' wide experience in working with a broad range of firms and agencies has been captured and translated into simple language and easily understood examples. Concepts are clearly covered and accompanied by practical guidelines that can be used by managers, researchers, evaluators, and others to help design and implement effective productivity measurement efforts in virtually any organization.

PREFACE

The struggle for improved productivity has never been more crucial than it is now, in the waning years of the twentieth century. Increased foreign competition in an expanding global economy, more efficient foreign industry using relatively cheap labor, rising costs of resources, and an aging industrial infra-structure have combined to deal productivity a staggering blow. In a nutshell, American industry is producing less, at higher costs. At the same time, the world's opinion of the quality of American goods has changed, and "Made in the U.S.A." no longer is a label meaning high quality. Though uncertainty remains the surest bet for the future, most economists, futurists, and other prophets of industry broadcast a clear message: improve productivity, or go out of business.

Efforts to improve productivity have been attempted in virtually all sectors of business and industry. In recent years we have seen a rash of programs and pronouncements aimed at curing productivity ills: quality circles, "Japanese management," worker participation in decision-making, statistical quality control, and "just-in-time" inventory methods are but a few of the efforts popular today.

Common among almost all of the productivity improvement strategies in use is measurement. Measurement is used to indicate whether there is a need for any improvement in the first place, is often a part of the improvement process itself, and is used to gauge whether improvement efforts are making any progress. Often, in fact, measurement alone has a dramatic impact on productivity since the effects of feedback are so powerful. Many sales managers have, for example, discovered that simply posting individual salesperson performance records in a visible place and on a regular basis has a demonstrable positive impact on sales performance.

Measurement of work performance and productivity is not only a common feature, but is critical to any improvement effort. Measurement helps diagnose productivity needs, and can be used to focus improvement resources on the most needy departments and operations. In a grocery distribution and retailing operation, for example, a simple measure of the labor hours needed to unload a boxcar of goods might be used to monitor unloading efficiency. When this measure falls over time, or is lower than industry standards, a productivity problem might exist, and can thus be further investigated. Monitoring of performance, feedback, and regular consideration of performance peaks and valleys as indicated by measurement data are powerful stimuli for change. Productivity improvement efforts cannot operate "blind." Measurement must be used to show where assistance is needed and where it is working so that improvement resources can be evaluated and re-allocated. Anyone seeking to increase productivity or assist with improvement programs must understand productivity measurement strategies and techniques, and should be proficient in designing measurement approaches.

This book shows how productivity can be measured and used for improvement in any business, industry, service, or social program operation. It especially focuses on measurement strategies that unit-level managers or researchers can use to assess performance in any particular part of a larger organization.

A driving principle of this book is that measurement strategies must be simple and practical. Measurement that is not easily developed, implemented, and understood by managers, evaluators, or researchers will not be used, and therefore will do nothing to improve performance. It is an inescapable fact, as well, that all efforts aimed at improving productivity run the strong likelihood that they will hurt productivity, for they take resources away from primary production or service. Workers who are, for example, attending a quality circle meeting to review the latest performance data are not at work on the line, and thus their labor is lost to production. For this reason, measurement strategies should be as simple as possible, use the least possible capital and labor resources, and should be an integral part of the primary work process. Thus, readers will find that this book pays particular attention to practicality and utility.

Productivity measurement is, of course, not new. American industry has been regularly measured for decades, and national productivity statistics are compiled and reported almost daily. Public Law 94-136, passed in the mid-1970s, established a national center for productivity inquiry; an early and major activity of this group was to sponsor a measurement conference held in Washington, D.C. in June, 1976 (National Center for Productivity and Quality of Working Life 1983). As well, staff economists and financial controllers in most businesses regularly measure and track business performance for consideration by top management. But productivity measurement has been almost the sole province of financial experts, economic consultants, and researchers. Only recently has productivity measurement been considered a responsibility of line management at the unit level. The practice of measurement at this level is found in only a few companies and agencies.

We believe that practical productivity measurement is a tool that should be accessible to all managers and researchers. Our consulting experience in a variety of performance improvement projects for a range of clients has convinced us that simple, useful measurement methods can have profound impact. We are convinced that these techniques can be learned and effectively used by almost all managers and researchers in any organization; one needs no advanced degree in research methods nor a mastery of complex statistical procedures to employ sound and effective measurement practices. This book is intended to provide a comprehensive and practical guide that should enable the reader to embark on a useful productivity measurement and improvement endeavor, seeking further technical assistance when needed through the many references included.

Managers and researchers in business, industry, service, or social and educational agencies should find this book useful to understand productivity measurement and learn the steps for designing and operating a productivity measurement improvement project for their own unit or operation. Students preparing to serve as managers, organizational development consultants, or applied researchers will find this book to be an effective introduction to the practice of productivity measurement. Consultants and other more experienced applied researchers should find sound, practical advice and techniques in these pages to expand their repertoire.

The book is organized into three areas of concern. Chapters 1, 2, and 3 present basic productivity measurement information; Chapters 4, 5, and 6 contain specific "how to" information for developing useful measures; Chapters 7 and 8 present practical steps and procedures for implementing productivity measurement schemes in organizations.

Chapter 1 relates productivity measurement to the larger context of organizational operation and improvement. It is, in part, an effort to bring order to the somewhat chaotic collection of productivity improvement approaches, methods, and fads. The function of productivity measurement in such current techniques as quality circles, statistical process control, and others, is defined, explained, and clarified. This first chapter shows how measurement serves the ultimate productivity goals of quality and profitability, and discusses a range of more immediate objectives to be served by productivity measurement. Readers will leave the first chapter with a concise understanding of what productivity measurement is, why it is useful, where and why it originated, and where it appears to be headed next. In addition, this chapter sensitizes readers to the important issues and problems confronting those who seek to measure and thereby improve productivity.

Chapter 2 explains the fundamental concepts and definitions needed to understand the practice of productivity measurement and forms the foundation for the chapters that follow. This chapter includes brief explanations and examples of some primary measurement concepts, such as validity, bias, and sampling methods with which productivity measurement practitioners should be familiar.

The authors define four essential criteria for successful productivity measurement applications in Chapter 3. Unfortunately, as the authors explain, many measurement efforts are driven mostly by concerns for *accuracy*. While accuracy is necessary, it alone will not bring success. This chapter explains how practitioners must seek measures that (1) focus on quality, (2) are integrated with organization goals and strategy, (3) are tied to the reward/punishment structure, and (4) are derived from extensive levels of employee involvement.

Chapter 4 explains methods and issues in measuring outputs: the results and products of activities. Many examples and alternative approaches are provided. This chapter especially emphasizes measuring outputs of service, professional, and "white collar" functions.

Chapter 5 is similar in structure and content to the previous chapter except that the focus is on measuring inputs. This chapter defines inputs as the resources consumed by an activity, or all the costs experienced in the production of outputs. Measurement procedures in this chapter, then, include methods for measuring effort as well as other tangible resources. Again, the emphasis is on practical measurement methods, especially those pertaining to service and professional functions. And, again, many examples and alternatives are provided.

No measures are useful in improving productivity if the measures cannot be readily used to "keep score" on improvement efforts. Thus, Chapter 6 gives the reader practical guidance in creating highly informative, clear, and "user friendly" measurement report formats and indices. Many alternatives, from simple ratios and trend reports to multiple measure matrices, are included. In all index formats the emphasis is on utility and clarity, so that the critical feedback function of a measure is optimized.

The final two chapters of the book are aimed at helping readers understand and execute the several steps and functions necessary to make a productivity measurement system work in a complex organization. Chapter 7 presents detailed steps and procedures, with examples and illustrations, for designing unit level productivity measures. These steps have been used successfully by the authors in their consulting work and are similar to those procedures used elsewhere in a number of major corporations. The steps begin with the analysis required to make certain that unit goals are integrated with the goals of the larger organization, proceed through the development of pertinent measures, and end with the construction of useful feedback indices.

Chapter 8 focuses not on the single unit level, but presents guidelines, procedures and considerations for making a productivity measurement effort work at the corporate or whole organization level. This chapter presents useful guidelines for gaining acceptance, establishing higher level management commitment, and other crucial elements a manager or consultant must strive to accomplish in order to facilitate a continuing and successful measurement effort. As in preceding chapters, the emphasis is on practicality, and generous illustrations and examples are provided.

1

Introduction to Productivity Measurement

This introductory chapter relates productivity measurement to the context of organizational operation and productivity improvement. It begins by looking at both the historical and current concepts and activities related to productivity measurement. The middle of the chapter presents an overview of current productivity measurement movements such as productivity centers, statistical process control, quality circles, the use of performance appraisals, "Japanese" management techniques, and performance engineering. The conclusion of the chapter discusses two specific areas. The first is the relationship of productivity measurement to organizational performance, especially quality and profitability. The second traces potential problems and pitfalls in productivity measurement. A listing of issues to be aware of when engaging in productivity measurement is provided.

THE NATURE OF PRODUCTIVITY MEASURES

Productivity has been a concern for as long as people have been engaged in work. Records from the remains of ancient ruins indicate that crop yields were charted from year to year; government officials, even in ancient times, were concerned with the productivity of farmers and the land. Productivity measurement, while not called by that name, was implicitly understood by farmers in the early days of this century. Prior to the use of mechanical farm equipment, farmers were solely dependent upon human labor for accomplishing farm work. As early U.S. farmers cleared more land and acquired productive farm acreage, additional labor was needed to complete all farm tasks. A relatively simple solution was to enlarge the family and create a greater pool of laborers. The farmers clearly understood that their farm output was dependent upon their labor input.

Time studies in the industrial age were undertaken to improve the output of the factory worker (Taylor 1947). The number of parts produced in a minute or an hour was carefully recorded by time study experts. These early studies viewed production as a process of labor and time inputs. Time study experts attempted to design jobs to speed up production processes, holding labor as a constant, by reducing the amount of time needed to produce the same number of parts in production. These early time and motion studies attest to a far ranging concern with productivity and a fascination with ideas that could squeeze more production out of given amounts of labor.

Even individuals in their daily lives are concerned with productivity measurement. A car buyer, for example, may check the gasoline mileage rating of a given car. That rating, expressed as miles per gallon (MPG), is simply a productivity measurement of the car's capability of turning gasoline into miles driven. For example, if the mileage rating of an automobile is 32 MPG, "32 miles" is an expression of the automobile's output where a single gallon of fuel is needed to produce the "32 miles."

THE DEFINITION OF PRODUCTIVITY MEASUREMENT

In a nutshell, productivity reflects results as a function of effort. When productivity improves, it means that more results are being gained for a given amount of effort. In a classical sense, productivity is defined as a ratio such that the output of an effort under investigation is divided by the inputs (labor, energy, and so forth) required to produce the output. Consider some examples. The number of bushels of corn can be seen as one key output of a farm operation. The farmer's time and labor could be considered the input. The number of parts produced by a production line worker might be output. The amount of time it takes for one laborer on the line to produce "x" number of parts might be input. Here are some further examples of productivity measures from a variety of settings:

$$\frac{\text{number of pages typed}}{\text{hours of secretarial time}} \qquad \frac{\text{number of freight cars unloaded}}{\text{number of laborers, lift trucks}}$$

$$\frac{\text{number of students instructed}}{\text{hours of instruction}} \qquad \frac{\text{number of customers helped}}{\text{number of customer service reps}}$$

$$\frac{\text{number of houses cleaned}}{\text{hours of maid service}} \qquad \frac{\text{number of parts produced}}{\text{amount of electrical energy consumed}}$$

Notice that each productivity measure is expressed as a ratio. For example, the productivity of a secretary would be measured as 20 when 20 pages (output) are typed with a single hour's labor (input). If the secretary took a speed typing course or used a new, high speed word processor, and as a result now typed 30 pages in one hour, the measure would become 30 (30 pages divided by 1 hour).

HISTORICAL ROOTS OF PRODUCTIVITY MEASUREMENT

The productivity of the American economy has been quantified in some form since the 1880s (Kendrick and Creamer 1961). It has only been since World War II that real attention has been paid to the topic, however. Today, most Americans are keenly aware of some aspect of productivity. Following World War II, interest in global markets and global economic development was slowly generated. Productivity information became critical to governments, business, and industry. If it was possible to produce a mouse trap for 75 cents an hour in labor in a third world country, the input labor costs for the mouse trap in a U.S. plant were, by comparison, very expensive. As manufacturing capacity increased, so the need for new markets to consume the output of those manufacturing processes likewise expanded. One result of new global competition and the growing concern for productivity was the formation in the 1950s of national productivity centers (Kendrick and Creamer 1961). In the 1960s, international productivity representatives began meeting; the first such international conference was held in Japan in 1983 ("Measuring Productivity" 1983).

Fueling current interest in productivity are the dual fires of the U.S. productivity stagnation in the 1970s and the coming global marketplace of the next century. The recession of the 1970s, the oil embargo, and the strength of foreign competition caused productivity issues to be looked at seriously. Suddenly, business-as-usual was no longer possible. Organizations understood that to remain competitive meant to be very productive. Survival and profitability were seen as a direct result of productivity (Miller 1984).

A recent and highly publicized concern for productivity can be found in the U.S. automotive manufacturing industry. As global competition began to erode U.S. manufacturers' market share, U.S. manufacturers discovered that simply *producing* cars no longer meant profits and survival. Suddenly, the issues of productivity, quality, and price became paramount to consumers. The United Auto Workers contract of 1987, for example, had two main ingredients: job security *and* worker productivity. It should be noted that one description of productivity includes the quality dimension. That is to say, producing an increased number of cars does not increase productivity. Finished products also have to surpass current quality levels: closer tolerance, better fit, fewer reworks, and so forth (Hayes 1985).

When gasoline prices skyrocketed in the 1970s, people became interested in the gasoline mileage of their automobiles. Foreign automakers were producing small, lightweight cars that produced superior gasoline mileage. Never before in the history of the automobile industry had the question of productivity been the major issue in the purchase of a car. Prior to this time, size, power, and comfort were a customer's main concerns. Suddenly, both the government and automakers became very interested in the productivity of the automobile.

When costs of production race ahead of an organization's ability to price its products profitably, productivity again becomes an issue. The paper manufacturing industry is currently experiencing this phenomenon. Because of national and international competition, paper manufacturers are unable to raise prices on their products. At the same time, their costs of production, through union negotiated salary increases and the cost of capital equipment improvements, have gone up dramatically. While the revenue from the sale of their outputs has remained essentially flat, their cost of inputs has risen significantly. Two major trends can be seen as a result of this productivity issue. Many paper companies are moving their operations to the southern part of the U.S. to get away from union environments and union pay scales. The second is that paper companies are locating their operations overseas, in Third World countries, where the costs of labor and overhead are significantly less than they would be in the U.S. As our world moves closer and closer to a global economy, few organizations will be unaffected by productivity issues in the future (Baumol and McLennan 1985).

Organizational leaders are those most often interested in productivity improvements. Yet, in the 1980s, union and management are sharing greater concern because it often means jobs retention and organization survival. Production concerns are now reaching the production worker level. No longer are productivity studies only the province of the accountant, plant manager, or vice president. New management techniques, such as "just-in-time" manufacturing, statistical process control, and work teams place responsibility for quality and productivity at the lowest levels of the organization.

Quality circles and statistical process control are increasingly common in manufacturing plants and other businesses across the U.S. Our experience in working with organizations using such techniques has been mixed, and we have seen many abuses of the basic principles of these potentially very powerful approaches. Quality circles are intended to be a mechanism for systematic employee problem-solving that use a variety of evaluative data and systematic group involvment procedures. Yet we have seen any number of quality circles that, for example, become gripe sessions based on personal agendas and subjective evaluations. Statistical Process Control (SPC) is a technique whereby workers at each step in production collect quality data for their particular operation. Then, these data are used to determine whether a process is "in control" (varying within acceptable range above or below a calculated mean). When a process goes "out of control," prescribed problem solving processes are employed and production halts. The aim of SPC is to engineer quality into the production process. Yet we have seen many instances where statistical data are collected, often very haphazardly, then left to collect dust while production goes on "as usual." When quality circles and SPC are used correctly, they collect measurement data on productivity and quality and use these data in prescribed, systematic applications for problem solving and decision making that can lead to tremendous productivity gains.

It seems likely that tomorrow's organizational leaders will need to understand productivity measurement very well and be able to teach it to others with ease. In addition, trainers, organization development consultants, and organization researchers will have to equip themselves with the skills and knowledge needed to measure, and understand, the productivity milieu.

EFFICIENCY, EFFECTIVENESS, AND PRODUCTIVITY

One concept related to productivity measurement is that of "effective" production and "efficient" production. Effective production is the process that produces the desired results. An organization might effectively produce more products or deliver more services. A dairy, for instance, might effectively produce 10% more ice cream on a weekly basis. A maid service might increase the number of houses cleaned by 15% on a monthly basis. In both cases, effective production has increased. However, those same effective increases in output may have been achieved at the cost of a much higher level of input. The additional 10% production of ice cream may have come at the price of a 15% increase in capital and a 12% increase in labor time. The 15% increase in homes cleaned may have come at the cost of a 20% increase in capital for automobile expenses and a 5% increase in direct labor costs. In these examples, while effective production has gone up, the overall productivity of the organization has gone down, simply because the inputs needed to produce the outputs have risen more quickly than the effective production. While both examples illustrate the achievement of desired effective production (increased outputs), the consumption of increased inputs has actually caused the organization to be less productive.

Efficient production would reflect achieving desired outputs with a minimum of inputs. That initially sounds like productivity at its maximum level. While efficiency and productivity are closely related, efficient production does not guarantee the best productivity. For instance, a clothing manufacturer might produce 100 sport coats a day, but do so with five fewer workers than was needed to produce those 100 units just a month ago. But if the reduction in labor input causes the defect rate in the sport coats to increase from 2 coats per 100 to 7 coats per 100, the business has gained nothing. In fact, the cost of rework or scrap rate may be higher than the reduced cost of input for the five fewer laborers. Note as well, that even if the defect rate is acceptable, the coats may be out of style or lack a sufficient range of sizes to be marketable, and so forth. If reduced labor costs also result in inferior quality, production may be more efficient, but time productivity will have suffered. Effectiveness and efficiency must go hand-in-hand in productive organizations. Organizations can temporarily survive without perfect efficiency; they usually die if they are ineffective, however.

A second related concept is that of working "harder" versus working "smarter." There are those who argue that productivity is not working harder, it is really working smarter. There is a difference between working harder and working smarter. Consider, for example, a swimmer who has trained very hard to achieve the peak of athletic condition. This swimmer can work no harder, for she has reached her maximum level of effort. But, if a clever coach can show her a new method of turning while swimming that reduces "dead time" in the water, and can train her to remain underwater longer on a dive (where hydrodynamic efficiency is greater), then the swimmer can reduce her race times without working any harder. Her level of effort during a race (input) will remain the same, but her race times (output) will improve, thus achieving a gain in productivity. The challenge for measurement practitioners is to help assess whether innovations in work methods and materials result in worthwhile productivity gains.

In recent years we have seen many uses of new technology and innovative approaches geared to "working smarter" in the manufacturing business. Reducing stockpiles of raw materials, thereby reducing storage costs, or using computers to schedule production to meet shipping demands (thereby reducing storage costs for finished products) are but two examples. We recently worked with a large, well-known manufacturer that produces home cleaning products. This company was producing units at its maximum capacity, with both machines and people working as hard as possible. Yet because their products were selling so rapidly, their manufacturing capabilities were not keeping up with their ability to sell their products. Obviously, working harder was not going to be a solution for this company. They decided that working smarter was the only way to increase their productivity; they couldn't work any harder. By rethinking and redesigning their manufacturing procedures, they were able to increase their production over a five-year period by nearly 40% with the same amount of input. One new procedure is "just-in-time" inventories, a system for keeping raw stock and finished goods at an absolute minimum (bringing in and shipping out the goods that were sold that day is the ideal). The other procedure is "reduced work-in-process," a system to eliminate batches of materials waiting to go from one process to the next (ideally, as a part comes out of one machine it goes immediately into the next). People who have applied these systems have found that their work effort has been reduced, but more critical was their increased ability to do critical thinking and problem solving (Simers, Priest, and Gary 1989).

Working smarter is not something that happens at the upper levels of management only. Bennis and Namus (1985), in their book on leadership, state that managers must empower people at the lowest levels in the organization to decide how they can best do their jobs. Empowering the people who know their work the best is one way of accomplishing "working smarter" objectives. Managers in all sorts of corporations realize that the people who best know how jobs could be done more efficiently are those who are doing those jobs right now. Empowering production workers to do those things that enable them to work smarter is a very powerful tool in increasing productivity.

Applied researchers, training professionals, and others have a key role to play in this "empowerment" process. As new approaches are tried out, action research should be pursued to assess results and help revise processes. When new techniques are developed and readied for widespread adoption, evaluation efforts should track implementation and impact so that ongoing adjustments and refinements can be made, and should assure that the feedback that workers need to keep productivity targets in the forefront is readily supplied.

WHY PRODUCTIVITY IS MEASURED

There are many particular needs and situations that precipitate productivity measurement efforts. But almost always, the long range purpose is to enhance productivity. Some of the more frequent applications we have noted in our practice are:

- Spotting productivity declines for "early warning"
- Comparing productivity across individuals, units, organizations, and industry to make management decisions
- Linking management and labor in productivity improvement efforts to build common awareness and responsibility
- Demonstrating productivity gains to interested stakeholders
- Conducting research and evaluation related to new or experimental methods
- Supporting incentive and bonus plans with objective productivity data

Companies that have taken productivity measurement and improvement seriously have found many benefits. An immediate benefit is the capacity to spot productivity declines at an early stage. Consider the example of a telemarketing representative whose measured number of outbound sales calls showed a drastic drop over a four-day period. The telemarketing supervisor was immediately able to determine that there was some sort of problem that needed addressing. By monitoring productivity data, the supervisor was able to address the problem before it became an entrenched way of operating for the telemarketing representative. In another situation, machine operators, using simple statistics to track the productivity of the machine they operated, noticed that the number of scrap pieces increased by 5% over a two-day period. Using these productivity measures, the operators knew that it was time to check dies or pressure settings so that scrap rates did not increase and could be returned to their previous low levels.

A second powerful application of productivity measurement is comparing productivity across individuals, work teams, organizations and competitors in like industries. A recent U.S. study ("Corporate scoreboard" 1988) compared profits per employee in identical industries. Some companies were shocked at the relatively low profits earned per employee. A grain milling operation discovered that it had the highest earnings per employee of any grain milling operation in the country. A pharmaceutical manufacturing house discovered that its earnings per employee were relatively low when compared to other pharmaceutical manufacturing companies. Each of these indices says something to management about overall organizational effectiveness, pricing of products, and profitability of operations.

Productivity measurement, when carried out by productivity teams made up of all levels of company employees, unites labor and management in seeking real productivity gains. In the industrial sector of the U.S. economy, most productivity gains are believed to be the responsibility of labor. Traditionally, it is perceived that management attempts to impact the productivity of the company through the union contract of the laborer. Organized labor has seen itself as carrying the weight of productivity and has rejected the idea that labor is totally responsible for productivity. When labor and management unite in productivity improvement efforts, sharing responsibility for the activities related to measuring, setting strategies for improvement, and rewarding those responsible for making improvements happen, a win-win situation is set up for both labor and management. Both have a stake in the process, both contribute, both are engaged in asking productivity questions and seeking solutions. While productivity data alone are not responsible for these cooperative successes, measurement has played a key role ("Bottom-up management" 1985).

Measuring productivity also gives an organization the evidence it needs to identify and celebrate gains. Individual work teams and units can be recognized for their growth and contribution to productivity. Consider the example of a small manufacturing organization with which we worked to establish a pilot team to accomplish several goals. One goal was to produce manufactured parts with zero defects, at a quantity greater than that which the individuals were currently producing, in such a way that the work team felt good about their contribution to the organization. As this work team found itself being very successful and productive, several positive results occurred. First, they were held up as models for the other new work teams that were being initiated. Second, they became the models and trainers for those involved in new work team efforts. And last, all team growth was celebrated company wide. Efforts such as these, now increasingly common, rely heavily on measurement data.

An increasing number of companies and organizations are struggling to develop plans to provide employee incentives and bonuses (Thomas and Olson, 1988). Many turn to productivity measurement schemes. Determining how the monies in such bonus plans are distributed is often difficult, however. Productivity measurement can make a significant contribution to determining how bonus plans are structured. Tying bonuses to productivity gains by the individual, the work unit, or even the entire organization, brings objectivity to the process. Tying the productivity of several levels in an organization to everyone's bonus encourages team work, cross-functional support, and ownership for organizational results.

SUMMARY

Efforts to gauge and control productivity have been around much longer than the term "productivity measurement," or even "productivity." And, despite the long history of productivity measurement and the sweeping technological changes over the past few centuries, the basics of productivity measurement have remained quite constant. The idea then, as is the idea now, is to figure out how much result is to be achieved for a given amount of effort. Yet, as was explained in the preceding text, there may be a number of more specific applications and expectations for the productivity measurement effort.

Despite the many applications of productivity measurement commonly found, it should be noted that all these variations are bound together by the single, overarching purpose of utility. Productivity is measured so that something can be done about productivity, either to detect and avoid lapses in productivity, to maintain worthwhile levels, or to improve less productive activities. This utilitarian purpose places a burden, then, on those researchers, managers, or others who seek to measure productivity.

Though the basic intent (assess, then improve productivity) is essentially simple, the process of implementing productivity measurement in today's organization is not so simple. In the context of the modern organization, its many bureaucratic layers, its concomitantly complex politics, and the existence of many non-production functions (personnel, legal affairs, and employee assistance, for instance) greatly complicate the effort. Add to this a variety of purposes, as explained in the preceding text, and the manager or organizational researcher is faced with a considerable task. Further, because productivity measurement often seeks to precipitate change, and change is inevitably threatening, productivity measurement requires deft handling of a number of complex, interrelated human relations and political concerns.

In the latter chapters of this book, we present information and advice that researchers, managers, and others who want to implement productivity measurement efforts should find useful. The earlier chapters deal more with the technical side of productivity measurement. In our experience, however, it is the human relations and political aspects that pose the biggest problems. This is not to say that the technical aspects are easy. Identifying critical inputs, defining operationally exact dimensions of output, and designing accurate measures are certainly problematic and pose a number of sophisticated technical issues. Yet our experience has been that our technical limits (and they are considerable) have rarely been stretched; we almost always design and use measures far less sophisticated than we could conceivably develop. In most cases, the resources available, the urgency of information needs, and the intolerance of the audience for anything smacking of complexity have combined to mitigate for technical simplicity.

2

Basics of Productivity Measurement

This chapter presents and discusses the basic elements and concepts underlying all measurement of productivity. It begins with the definition of the components of productivity measures: outputs, inputs, processes, and interim outputs from which all measures of productivity are built. This is true from the highest industry level to the smallest, individual operation level. These components include a definition of the fundamental concept, "customers," necessary to planning and conducting effective measurement programs. The middle part of this chapter discusses the basic output-to-input relationships that constitute improvement of productivity and presents an overview of the general types of productivity measures commonly used. The chapter closes with a review of some basic measurement concepts and issues, including validity and reliability, with which anyone engaged in productivity measurement must be familiar.

ELEMENTS OF PRODUCTIVITY MEASURES

As was noted in the preceding chapter, a productivity measure is a ratio that compares *output* (production of some desired result) with *input* (consumption of some defined resources). The example discussed in the first chapter demonstrated that the expression of "miles per gallon" could be construed as a productivity measure, wherein an automobile produces a given amount of miles (output) per some measured consumption of fuel (input). The "productivity" of the automobile under consideration would, in this example, be designated as a ratio comparing its production of the desired output (miles driven) to gallons of fuel consumed. Or, as another example, a consulting company might construct a measure to show how much secretarial resource (inputs) is expended to produce reports to clients (outputs). Briefly, this is what productivity measurement is all about: designing and using practical ratios to reflect the efficiency with which various outputs of interest are created.

Outputs

It is important to note in the familiar "miles per gallon" example, however, that a range of other outputs might have been considered and defined. Using this example, we can proceed to a more complete discussion of the concept of *output*. An automobile is typically driven with a particular purpose, or purposes, in mind. We might drive for pleasure, to transport goods from one place to another, to transport ourselves from one place to another, to feel the exhilaration of speed, and so forth. Each of these purposes implies a more complete consideration of output, or results. Consider, for instance, a salesperson who uses a car to transport himself and many boxes of heavy customer samples from place to place. In this case, a more useful index of productivity might be "amount of goods transported × number of miles per gallon of fuel." This more complete and particular expression of productivity will be more useful to the salesman than the general expression of "miles per gallon," since a smaller car capable (when unloaded) of attractive mileage might, when heavily loaded, consume inordinate amounts of fuel, be uncomfortable, or even unsafe. In this example, the output is defined more specifically as "amount of goods transported safely and comfortably."

In practical productivity measurement, an output always represents some unit of production, or results, of special interest. Here are some typical outputs the authors have defined in the course of helping others build useful measures:

- number of contracts negotiated
- number of mean ratings earned over 4.5 on a 5 point scale
- amount of profit per completed contract
- number of forms completed
- number of client diagnostic profiles completed without error
- amount of pleasurable reaction expressed
- number of parts produced meeting quality specifications
- gallons of extract with no impurities or residues produced
- number of clients seen

Reviewing this list of some typical outputs, we can identify key points crucial to a complete understanding of the concept of *output* as it is used in productivity measurement.

1. Each output is expressed as a quantity (number, amount, gallons, and so forth). Identification of some unit of quantity is, of course, necessary for measurement.

2. Some of the outputs have a qualitative expression attached to them, such as ". . . meeting quality specifications," ". . . without error," or ". . . with no impurities or residues." These dimensions of quality further define each output. When the measures are implemented, only those outputs that meet the specified quality criteria will be counted. When assessing the productivity of a maple sugar operation, for example, we counted as output only the gallons of syrup that were pure enough for marketing. As was discussed in the previous chapter, it is misleading and counter-productive to "count" defective outputs in productivity ratios, because outputs not meeting quality specifications require more work (input) to repair, to "make them fit for consumption."

   In almost all instances, it is imperative that a quality dimension be defined for each output. Rarely is it useful to merely count quantity of production, as such outputs, when incorporated into a ratio, will not reflect true productivity.

3. Some outputs will be tangible goods, such as "forms," or "parts;" other outputs may represent services, such as "clients seen;" sometimes, outputs might be expressed as subjective reactions, as in the example from the list above: "amount of pleasurable reaction expressed" (this example comes from measuring the effectiveness of various amusement park rides). Outputs represent desired *results*, and thus are not always and only tangible, "hard" goods.

4. In any and all cases, identification of outputs to be used in productivity assessment *requires and assumes measurement*. An obvious instance of this fact, from the preceding list of sample outputs, is "number of mean ratings received over 4.5 on a 5 point scale." This example comes from a case in which training workshop leaders' abilities to earn favorable trainee reactions were an output (result) of interest. Here, the output clearly requires measurement (in this case, a trainee reaction rating scale), and a means of aggregating and analyzing earned scores for each training leader. Not so obvious examples on the list of outputs are "forms completed" or "clients seen." It can be quickly seen, however, that we would need some rules for defining and then counting which forms are completed, or which clients have, in fact, been seen. Will a form with a blank space, for example, be counted as "complete"? If a client attends, but leaves a session early because the counselor has an emergency, will we count this as an instance of a client "seen"?

   Measurement requires rules for assigning events (Landy, Zedeck, and Cleveland 1983) or objects (outputs) to categories ("seen," "completed," and so forth). Readers with some background in measurement will recognize the need to "operationalize variables," which in the case of productivity measurement means that you have to have clear-cut rules and procedures for deciding which outputs meet conditions to be included as a "real" output, and which do not.

5. Deciding on which outputs are to be used in a productivity ratio, and just how to operationally define those outputs, is a crucial step in productivity measurement. Typically, however, this step is not carefully executed, and many productivity measurement efforts have gone astray, with the result that resources are invested in measuring the wrong things. Even though the latter chapters of this book show how to decide just what outputs to measure, we raise the topic here because it is so important.

Customers

The concept of "customer" is integral to productivity measurement even though the customer does not appear in the measure itself (the only elements of a productivity ratio are outputs and inputs). In constructing practical productivity measures, any unit or operation of an organization has its own customers—the people or units who use what the operation produces.

Customers are not only the ultimate buyers or consumers of some product or service. Take the example of a grocery store: Obviously there are customers who go to the store to shop and buy food. Now consider the accounting operation in the store. This operation provides important information (data about profits, expenses, and so forth) to the manager, a customer of this operation, and to the owner—another customer of this operation. In productivity measurement, "customers" are the people or operations that consume, or otherwise need and use, the product or results of an operation. Since any operation in an organization presumably has a purpose, it therefore has "customers." If no one, or no other operation, has any use for what an operation produces (if it has no customers), then the operation has no function and should not exist!

Sometimes identifying the customers of an operation can be difficult, and requires considerable analysis. Later, in Chapter 7, we provide examples and guidelines to reduce this difficulty.

There are two important reasons why "customers" must be identified and considered. First, identifying customers helps to clarify which outputs of a unit are most important, and thus should be measured to improve productivity. (Chapter 7 expands this process in greater detail). Secondly, *quality* characteristics tie the customers to an operation or unit. Customer needs and expectations are the basis from which quality criteria are derived. In fact, one common definition of quality is "fit for use by the customer." The quality of parts produced by a supplier to an automobile manufacturer, for example, is determined by the specifications (for tolerances, finish, durability, hardness, and so forth) set by the auto manufacturer (the customer), who cannot use any parts failing quality specifications.

Customer expectations, needs, and opinions for quality form the basis for specifying measurable quality criteria that will be incorporated into the output component of the productivity ratio. For this reason, thinking about, identifying, and interacting with customers is a crucial part of productivity measurement.

Throughputs

The student of productivity measurement will sometimes encounter the term "throughput." A throughput is, in fact, an output. But it is a special sort of output that is intended for internal consumption. For example, a wash and waxing operation might identify a cleaned and waxed car as its primary output; an output provided to customers who purchase a service for their dirty automobiles.

If the carwash operation is analyzed into sub-operations, we can identify the sub-operation that involves washing the car before it is passed on to the next major sub-operation, waxing. This relationship between sub-operations is depicted graphically below:

WASH CAR → WAX CAR

In this example, a "washed car" is a throughput—the output of an internal sub-operation that is, in turn, provided as an input to a later sub-operation. As can be seen, the throughput is, in fact, an output. For the carwash, this throughput quality is critical to meeting customer expectations.

This throughput example (a washed car) could be quite critical to improving the productivity of the carwash. In this example, the washing operation is probably relatively expensive, consuming a major portion of the carwash's resources. And, the quality of the throughput is very important to the overall output: a customer with a thoroughly cleaned and waxed car. If the washing operation is not effective, then overall output quality suffers dramatically, as few customers will be satisfied with a dirty car, even if it happens to be properly waxed.

Identification of critical throughputs is often an important function in productivity measurement and improvement efforts, because, as the carwash example simply illustrates, there is often considerable productivity leverage to be gained by measuring and improving the quality or efficiency of throughputs. Later chapters in this book will further discuss the notion of throughputs.

Inputs

"Inputs" is the term we use to define the resources consumed in the production of outputs. Thus, inputs include all the tangible resources consumed (materials, supplies, and so forth), the services that support production (heat, light, space, rentals, computer time, and so forth), and the effort or labor of people who use these resources to actually produce the output. Even though the term "input" includes all these various resources and expenses, typical productivity measures commonly use only one, or a few, major inputs. When, for example, we assess the efficiency of an automobile by measuring "miles per gallon," the input portion of this measure is only fuel consumed; this measure does not include the effort (labor) needed to drive the auto, wear on tires, oil consumption, and the many other resources actually consumed in driving a car from one place to another. This inclusion of only some resources will be discussed later in this chapter when we look at "partial" versus "total" measures.

Here are some inputs commonly used in a variety of measures:

- secretarial time
- labor hours
- computer time
- capital equipment
- consulting services
- energy (electricity, for example)
- management time
- total division budget
- writing supplies
- labor, overhead, and energy costs

Again, the reader should take care to notice several points about this list of typical inputs. First, as was the case with outputs, inputs must be measurable and quantifiable. The identification of each input (secretarial time, for example) constitutes a category, and necessitates rules for assigning phenomena to that category. Will we include as "secretarial time," for instance, the costs of relaxation and bathroom breaks that occur while a secretary produces a report? If a manager uses her computer to prepare a draft of the report before giving it to the secretary, is that counted as "secretarial time"? The consumption of inputs will also necessitate a procedure for measuring (counting, documenting, aggregating, and so forth) the actual expenditure of resources. Secretaries might, for example, keep a log of time spent on each report. Or, they might indicate an estimate of how much time they spent, or the unit might simply calculate "secretarial labor" as the clerical budget for the unit. (Deciding which sort of measurement procedure is most appropriate is dealt with later in this chapter).

It should also be noted that some inputs from the preceding list are very specific and minor (writing supplies, for example), while others are much more broad and inclusive, such as "labor," or "energy." Whether inputs are defined very narrowly, or very broadly, depends on what kinds of productivity elements a measure has been created to monitor and control. If it is felt that writing supplies are a major cost element, and it is further felt that these costs are wildly out of control, then perhaps "writing supplies" is an appropriate input for inclusion in a productivity ratio.

Levels of Analysis

Productivity measurement can be carried out for an entire organization, entire industries, or even entire countries. At the other end of the spectrum, the productivity of very microscopic operations within larger operations can be measured. We have measured, for example, the productivity of the procedure in which telemarketing personnel complete the first 30 seconds of a telephone transaction with a customer.

Regardless of the level of analysis, from whole country to microscopic operation deep within an organization, the same principles apply: outputs and output quality are measured, and are compared (through a numerical ratio) to measured input consumption. It is crucial, however, that productivity measurement facilitators recognize the differences amongst the many levels within the organization where they carry out their work, and that they recognize the level where they are in fact operating.

The primary focus of this book is on the "unit" level within a larger organization. We have defined "unit" as the smallest functional work group within an organization. Thus, a unit is comprised of several jobs that are almost always held by a number of job incumbents, and is presided over by a person with unit managerial responsibility. Sometimes, productivity measurement efforts might focus on operations within the unit that have been identified as a result of analysis, wherein the unit operations are subdivided into two or more components, each with its own processes, inputs, and outputs. When sub-unit level operations are analyzed and measured, great care must be taken to make sure that the sub-operations measured are, in fact, important for overall unit productivity. Later, we will define the threat of "sub-optimization," which occurs when the productivity of sub-operations have been improved, but the improved operations have little bearing on overall unit productivity. Where there is confusion about what level one is operating at, the threat of sub-optimization looms large. The researcher must also carefully select the levels to be measured. Measurement at the wrong level can cause findings to be inaccurate and misleading.

Productivity measurement at the unit level must also be concerned with levels above it. If, for example, we were measuring the productivity of a training unit within a large company, we will have to identify the internal and external customers of this unit. Identification of customers will take us "outside" of the training unit, to other units and larger divisions within the company, and to units and organizations outside the company. Understanding who these customers are, and how they relate to the training unit, is important, and requires analysis of operations above and outside the unit level.

Later, in Chapter 7 and 8, we return to the concept of levels of analysis when we discuss procedures for creating productivity measures.

HOW PRODUCTIVITY RATIOS
REFLECT PRODUCTIVITY IMPROVEMENT

There are five (5) basic ways in which ratios reflect changes in productivity. In discussing each of these five ways, we will refer to the same example: the number of secretarial hours of effort consumed in producing reports for clients, such as in a consulting firm that has a costly and elaborate production process. We would express this measure in a ratio as:

$$\frac{\text{number of acceptable reports produced}}{\text{secretarial hours expended for reports}}$$

Assume that each extensive report consumed four hours of secretarial time during a one month period. After the secretaries were given special training in using report layout templates, each report consumed only three and one half hours. Producing the same output, while consuming less resources, represents a productivity gain.

Another way in which productivity might increase is when more reports are produced while the amount of labor stays the same. That is, the secretaries might work no more this month than they did last month, but their productivity increases (perhaps they work faster, or have to make fewer corrections), and they turn out more reports.

The third basic productivity relationship occurs when both input and output increase, but output increases faster than input. Perhaps the secretaries produce 20% more reports, but use only 10% more effort.

The fourth productivity relationship occurs in a similar fashion when output and inputs both decrease, but outputs decrease *less* than inputs. For instance, if the secretaries produce 10% fewer reports, but do so with 20% less effort, then again we have a productivity gain.

The fifth and final productivity gain relationship represents the hotly pursued (and elusive!) ideal when *more* output is produced, but *less* input is used. Assume, for example, that the company in our example also leases secretarial services whenever it has reports to get out to clients. These secretaries type more quickly and accurately, since they are word processing specialists, *and* they cost less per hour than the permanent staff. Thus, the firm gets more reports, for less secretarial expense.

GENERAL TYPES OF MEASURES

There are some general types of productivity measures with which the practical practitioner and researcher should be familiar. These different types of measures are all commonly encountered, but each has special uses, and each has special limitations.

Partial Versus Total Measures

The first major difference between productivity measures is one of scope. There are "total" measures and there are "partial" measures. (National Center for Productivity and Quality of Working Life 1983) The distinction between total and partial measures relates entirely to the level of analysis. That is, a total measure reflects productivity at the whole organization level, and a partial measure reflects productivity at some level lower than the entire organization. A total measure for a commercial fast food operation, for example, might be:

$$\frac{\text{total sales}}{\text{total costs}}$$

Not that there could be other total measures as well, such as:

$$\frac{\text{number of satisfied customers}}{\text{annual expenses}}$$

or

$$\frac{\text{amount of food served}}{\text{total annual costs}}$$

Each of these is a total measure because it (a) is intended to reflect overall productivity, and (b) it incorporates a comprehensive measure of inputs (total cost, for example).

A partial measure for the same fast food operation could be:

$$\frac{\text{number of satisfied customers}}{\text{labor expenses}}$$

This would be a partial measure because it incorporates only one particular kind of input. This sort of partial measure, like the total measures, intends to reflect overall productivity, but it isolates a particular resource, so that changes in the expenditure of that resource can be tracked, and the impact of these changes on apparent productivity can be assessed. The risk of using a partial measure such as this is that it could give a misleading estimate of true productivity. If, for example, labor costs went down, but costs for materials skyrocketed, the measure reflects a productivity gain, even though real productivity may have suffered because of increased material costs. In general, however, where the partial measure accounts for the expenditure of a major, controllable resource, then it provides very useful information.

Here is another partial measure:

$$\frac{\text{number of satisfactory hamburgers cooked}}{\text{amount of grill electrical power used}}$$

Notice that this measure isolates a very minor output (cooked hamburgers) and also a relatively minor input. Obviously, this measure relates only to a particular sub-operation (cooking hamburgers on the electric grill), and thus is useful only for modifying either the number of satisfactory hamburgers, or the amount of electrical power consumed. The measure is "partial" in two ways: (1) it measures a sub-operation's output, and (2) it measures only a single input.

Consider this example:

$$\frac{\text{number of satisfactory hamburgers cooked}}{\text{total costs for hamburger cooking}}$$

This could now be considered a "total" measure for the sub-operation of hamburger cooking, in that it incorporates a measure of all the resources expended to produce the sub-operation's output. Such a measure is useful, again, only for improving the productivity of this particular sub-operation. Yet, it gives a reliable estimate of the total productivity of this sub-operation. If the measure incorporated only some of the inputs expended in hamburger cooking versus all of them (cooking oil, labor, and power, for example), it remains a partial measure.

Partial measures can also be added to create aggregate measures of productivity. An example could be:

$$\frac{\text{total number of satisfactory hamburgers cooked}}{\text{electricity used } + \text{ labor hours } + \text{ cost of grill}}$$

As long as the denominator contains less than all the resources used to create the output, it remains a partial measure. "Aggregate" partial measures are especially useful when the output is heavily dependent on several inputs. It is also easy to disaggregate any measure. In the example above, it would be easy to break out the formula to determine the productivity of labor or the grill or electricity alone.

It is important to understand the concept of total and partial measures. Partial measures are often much more useful than total measures, because they isolate one, or a few, inputs or outputs. Thus, they help to understand the role of discrete inputs as they impact productivity, and thus enable fine level adjustments and improvements in operations.

Single Versus "Family" Measures

Measuring productivity, as in measuring anything, involves reduction. The science of measurement requires that large, complex phenomena be "reduced" to objective, operational, and measurable dimensions that will submit to quantitative expression. For this reason, any productivity measure is somehow "less" than the phenomenon of the productivity the measure aims to represent.

The productivity of a hamburger stand, for instance, can be numerically expressed as:

$$\frac{\text{number of hamburgers sold}}{\text{resources expended}}$$

This measure reduces the entire concept of productivity at the hamburger stand to a single, narrow number: the quantity of hamburgers sold. This number says nothing about what might perhaps be some other important goals of the owner of this hamburger stand. Perhaps, for example, the owner of the hamburger stand is also interested in providing a safe and happy location for birthday parties for neighborhood children, wishes to build the net worth of his hamburger stand's real estate so that he can sell it and retire on the proceeds, and wishes, as well, to provide training opportunities at his business for local high school students. None of these other intended results (outputs) are accommodated by the single measure: number of hamburgers sold divided by total resources expended.

In this example, the owner has a few choices. He can forego his other interests, recognizing that these interests are secondary to his primary goal of selling hamburgers, and thus making a profit to enable progress toward his other goals, Or, he could hire a measurement expert to construct an elaborate formula to combine all of his interests into one mesaure. Or, he could use several measures—one for each of his major interests. Such a group of measures is called a "family" of measures, in that they are each separate entities, but they are related to one another. Together, they represent the entire interest of the owner (or, to continue our family analogy, the head of the family!). This family of measures might include:

$$\frac{\text{number of meaningful training opportunities}}{\text{percentage of gross sales spent on training}}$$

$$\frac{\text{number of hours of use of birthday party room}}{\text{percentage of budget dedicated to birthday room}}$$

$$\frac{\text{annual increase in net worth of property}}{\text{annual costs of capital improvements}}$$

$$\frac{\text{number of hamburgers sold}}{\text{total expenses}}$$

The four measures in this "family" now account for a far greater proportion of the complete goals for this particular business; more of what this business is all about is represented by the measures. And, because the measures each represent a specific and discrete output, the owner is better able to track the performance of each output, whereas combining them into a single measure would have masked the contribution of each of the elements. A single measure might show an overall increase. But this overall increase could result from a great increase in sales, overriding a decrease in the number of birthday parties.

A family of measures clearly provides more, and more discrete, information about total unit performance than a single measure, and thus is more compatible with decision making in a context where trade-offs are common. Use of the family of measures precludes the ability to reference a single performance measure, and thus a response to the question "How is the unit doing?" will always be qualified. Our hamburger shop owner might respond, for example:

Well, sales are a little down. Birthday parties are about the same, but net worth on the property is way up because of all the goodwill we've generated with our party room, and since we had so many trainees last summer. Overall, I feel pretty good about things. I'm not getting any younger, and I really need that retirement assurance and I really don't need so much income these days, what with the wife's social security. Then again, it'd be nice to get sales up, since our kid is headed to college this year. I guess, all things considered, we're doing okay. And, it sure is nice to see those new kids learn how to get by at a real job. That warms my heart, I can tell you.

Where there is a rigid demand for a single, unitary indicator of performance, a single measure is clearly the choice. But, as our hypothetical hamburger owner's response shows, we believe that single measures rarely, if ever, reflect the true state of things, as there are always multiple interests, goals, and values. For these reasons, a family of measures typically provides more utility.

GENERAL MEASUREMENT CONCERNS

Productivity measurement requires attention to a number of generic measurement concerns, as would measurement of any type in any social setting. And, measurement is a highly technical and often complex task and may require expertise beyond the repertoire of the typical manager (Landy et al., 1984; Brinkerhoff et al., 1983; Campbell and Stanley, 1966). This book does not aim to expand the reader's repertoire of such technical knowledge and skills. But we do include a brief discussion of the most salient measurement concerns so that these concerns will not be overlooked. We do this so that users of this book will be reminded to seek additional expertise when they think they are swimming in waters deeper than the reach of their technical expertise.

Validity

Validity refers to the relationship between what is measured and what the person doing the measurement wants to know. If, for example, we want to know how marketable this book is (is it likely to sell?), it would be *less* valid to measure a productivity expert's opinion of the book than it would be to measure a typical manager's or beginning researcher's opinion. On the other hand, if we needed to know how current and sound the content of the book is, then the typical manager's or new researcher's opinion would be less valid than the expert's opinion. In more technical language, validity will be determined by the "fit" between the variable measured (a manager's opinion) and the construct about which we wish to make an inference (the book's marketability).

In productivity measurement, validity will be determined by whether the data collected through measurement are, in fact, related to phenomena that can be controlled to improve productivity. If, for example, a unit manager measures something that has very little relationship to what that unit really ought to be doing for the organization, then clearly what is measured will not help, and may hurt, productivity. Likewise, if a measure intends to measure a critical output, but in fact measures something else, again there is poor validity.

Consider these examples: Measuring how much a manager actually uses an accounting report would be a more valid indicator of the report's utility than would be a measure of the report's adherence to standard guidelines for organization and readability. Measuring how successfully a newly hired employee actually performs during the first six months on the job is a more valid assessment of the success of the hiring process than a rating of how closely the new employee's credentials matched the job description. A measure of how much and how well a trainee performs on the job is a more valid measure of training's effectiveness than is an end-of-workshop opinion about training's quality.

Arriving at valid measures initially requires careful and thorough consideration of just what it is that we want to know about in the first place. When we want to know how productive a training unit is, for example, we will have to carefully define what it is that this unit is supposed to produce in the first place: learning? job performance? satisfaction? loyalty and commitment? profits? The foundation for valid productivity measurement is laid when *outputs* are identified and their relationship to unit mission is assessed. If there is lack of agreement, imprecision, or confusion about outputs and missions, then measures based on these outputs are likely to raise serious concerns about validity.

The relationship between a unit's identified outputs, and the unit's "true" productivity, is one sort of validity that productivity investigators have to be concerned with. Another type of validity comes from the relationship between the measuring tool (a survey, an observation form, and so forth) and what it is that the tool aims to measure. Consider, for example, that we are interested in the productivity of a staff development function. Assume, for the sake of this example, that the output sought from this unit is improved job skill and knowledge. This output was thoughtfully identified and justified in terms of the long range goal of reducing employee turnover, on the premise that employees who receive effective job-knowledge training tend to remain longer with the organization. Now, assume that the measure chosen is a self-report survey of trainees administered at the end of each training session. Such a measure (asking trainees for beliefs about how much they think they learned) might be invalid (not really measuring the amount learned) because it is heavily influenced by how entertaining and exciting the training session was. That is, the tool *aims* to measure knowledge acquired, but might *really* measure entertainment value, and thus is not a valid measure of learning. A more valid measure might be a test of knowledge, given to the trainee when leaving the training, or an evaluation tool used by the trainee's supervisor to rate the trainee's job knowledge after training, or an opinion survey administered a few weeks after the session (after the initial "high" created by an entertaining session has subsided).

Perhaps the greatest threat to validity is the phenomenon known as "suboptimization." This occurs when the productivity of a minor function within a larger operation is improved, but the resultant gain in productivity for the larger operation is unaffected, or affected adversely. For example, consider a mail order catalog clothing retailer. One of the functions in this business is to open envelopes containing customer orders. Now, it would be possible to study this operation, measure its productivity (how long it takes to open envelopes, and so forth), and probably one could improve the speed and efficiency of this process. But, the envelope-opening procedure accounts for only a tiny fraction of the business's overall operations; improving the envelope opening process by even cutting its input consumption in half (opening twice as many envelopes with the same resources) will make hardly a dent in *overall* business productivity. Worse yet, all the effort expended on this relatively inconsequential activity probably could detract from overall productivity.

Within the context of the envelope-opening process, the measures used may be quite valid; that is, the measures may validly reflect important envelope-opening variables. But, only when the context of the larger organization is considered, do we see the envelope-opening process for what it really is—a minor, bit-player in the grander scheme of things. For this reason, true productivity validity demands that the manager or researcher take careful pains to see the "big picture," and avoid the dangerous suboptimization trap.

There are many measurement articles and books that discuss the topic of validity in great depth. Some good information can be found in the reference section at the end of this book. Readers are cautioned to carefully consider validity issues, and advised to seek more information as needed.

Reliability

Reliability describes the accuracy of a measure. A weight scale, for example, whose moving parts are worn and rusty, will give varying readings even though the same amount of weight is placed on it each time. Or, assume that a computer assistance unit wishes to measure its productivity in terms of how useful its services are to its customers in meeting their information needs. If the survey form it uses to assess customer opinion includes several confusing and poorly worded items, then it is likely to reflect opinions inaccurately and to be answered inconsistently by individuals who may, in fact, hold the same opinions.

Reliability is derived from characteristics of measuring tools and procedures. When measuring tools and procedures are poorly designed or not carefully administered, then inaccurate data are produced. We might have, for example, an extremely well-designed survey instrument that has been shown to be a very accurate and consistent measure of employee attitudes. However, one manager distributes it to employees in the company mail, another conducts a special group administration session with a lot of discussion about instrument items, another gives it only to a few selected employees, and yet another mails it to employees' homes. Given the inconsistency of administration, the data aggregated from all these instruments is likely to be an inaccurate index of the typical employee's attitudes, because different groups of employees responded from different perspectives and under different conditions. Thus, the reliability of the index is questioned.

Reliability is a characteristic of the measuring tool and the manner in which it is implemented. It relates to how well the measure consistently measures the same subject being studied. Accuracy, and thus high reliability, will come from careful design, field testing, redesign, and thorough, consistent administration of productivity measures. In summary, validity is not a characteristic of the measuring tool itself. Rather, it comes from the relationship between what a tool measures, and what one wants it to measure. It clarifies what the subject of measurement is. A measuring tool can be valid for one purpose, but not for another. In productivity measurement, validity concerns are addressed primarily through the process of identifying outputs and inputs for measurement, and justifying the identification through a careful analysis of mission and organization.

The distinction between reliability and validity can be illustrated as follows. A scale is used to determine the weight of objects. The scale indicates that a quantity of nails weighs 1 pound when, in fact, it weighs 15 ounces. It also indicates that a quantity of feathers weighs 1 pound when, in fact, it weighs 17 ounces. We would say the scale is not a *reliable* measure of weight. If the density of the quantity of feathers or nails was being measured, the scale would not indicate either. The scale is not a *valid* measuring instrument to indicate density.

It is possible for a measure to be reliable without being valid. An accurate scale may measure a pound reliably, but if density is the desired measure, it is still invalid. In order for a measure to be valid, however, it must be reliable. If a weight is the desired measure, then a scale might be a valid instrument to use. If it measures unreliably, however, it also makes the measure invalid.

Bias and Sampling

Bias can creep into measures unless samples drawn for measurement are carefully considered. We once arrived at a very inaccurate conclusion about customer satisfaction with a management information service, for example, because the instrument used to rate satisfaction was included *at the end* of a package of presumedly helpful materials provided to customers by the service unit. Returns of the instrument indicated high degrees of satisfaction. Yet, anecdotal information received by several unit workers indicated that many customers were not pleased. Some follow-up inquiry with survey non-respondents indicated that customers who were dissatisfied with the service never made it to the end of the package, and thus never completed or returned the instrument. We received returns only from satisfied customers, but most customers were, in fact, dissatisfied!

Careful and thoughtful sampling is crucial to avoiding bias. A process for assessing quality of manufactured parts, for example, that inspects only parts made on the day-shift will probably give a biased view of overall quality of production, since, historically, quality declines on the second and third shifts. Here are some more examples of biased samples: Trainees who are surveyed at the closing of a workshop will represent a biased sample, because those who did not like the session probably left early. Company cafeteria customers will probably rate service as acceptable, because those who think the cafeteria gives poor service eat elsewhere.

The preceding paragraph relates some of the more obvious examples of bias. Sampling errors can be more subtle and insidious, nonetheless creating bias. Consider a client rating form that asks recipients of company counseling services to assess the quality of those services. Further assume that these clients have some favorable reactions as well as some unfavorable reactions. Yet, the measuring instrument and data collection process may collect (sample) only positive opinions, for a variety of reasons: perhaps the instrument used contains more items reflecting ("begging") positive reactions; perhaps the culture of the organization suppresses negative expressions about anything; perhaps the clients fear that negative reactions will somehow be discovered and used against them.

There can be a number of forces that bias the way in which a person responds. As was the case with reliability, careful and thoughtful design, consideration, and redesign of data collection processes will help assure that each method is equally sensitive to the full range of possible responses and opinions. When using interview methods, for example, careful training of interviewers can help avoid the classic tendency of interviewees, because of subtle and even unconscious reactions they may perceive on the part of the interviewer, to bias their responses. Very often, interviewees say not what they really believe, but what they believe the interviewer wants to hear.

Reactivity

The tendency of a measuring process to influence what it measures is known as reactivity. That is, something about how the measurement is conducted influences the results. We once worked in a company, for example, that asked managers to submit samples of performance assessment reports they had completed so that the company could assess how well its new performance appraisal process was working. It was soon discovered that some managers were (probably out of fear of reprisal for failure to use the procedure) preparing report forms especially for submission—actually rewriting the reports they had really used in performance appraisal, then sending these re-written reports on to the employee relations division to be used in the measurement process.

This rather blatant example of reactivity was clearly not producing the right sort of data for making decisions about how well the new procedure was going. The measurement purposes would have been better served had actual performance appraisal reports been sampled. The measurement rule of thumb is that available data are far better than data manufactured for purposes of measurement. Measuring actual indicators of morale (grievance frequency, disputes with managers, and so forth) is superior to gathering survey data about how people feel about morale, for example. The rule of using available data has two important bases. First, already existing data are cheaper than data that result from new measurement procedures created just for the productivity assessment purpose. Secondly, available data are already there, and are thus not subject to being misrepresented, intentionally or otherwise.

SUMMARY

This chapter has presented and discussed some of the key definitions, issues, and concepts encountered in productivity measurement. The basic building blocks of productivity measurements were defined as measures of outputs and inputs. The concept of quality, and its inherent ties with productivity, were noted as part of the discussion of outputs, since measurement of output quantity alone can lead quickly to misrepresentations of productivity. The concept of *customer* was also raised in relationship to outputs and quality. Measures must be constructed with a number of issues in mind. Ignoring reliability, validity, bias, and reactivity will result in misleading measures.

3

Beyond Accuracy:
What Makes Successful Measures

It is a basic tenet, one with which we agree, that a productivity measure must be accurate. That is, a measure of productivity must truthfully and consistently reflect variations in actual productivity. Meeting the accuracy requirement is primarily a technical issue, and one that we think is not terribly difficult, given the current state of the measurement art and the plethora of literature describing techniques and examples. But measures must be more than simply accurate if they are to be constructively used in a complex organizational setting. In this chapter, we identify, describe, discuss, and illustrate four criteria that must be achieved if measures are to be successfully adopted as part of a continuing process of productivity improvement. In our opinion, these four criteria are more crucial than accuracy considerations. A measure that meets the four criteria we identify will result in helpful productivity improvements even if the measure is not very accurate.

We begin with a brief definition of each of the criteria. Then, the remainder of the chapter discusses each of the criteria more thoroughly and illustrates by way of various examples how that criterion impacts on productivity improvement.

THE FOUR CRITERIA FOR MEASUREMENT EFFECTIVENESS

The four criteria we define reflect very directly our bias toward utility. Above all, we believe productivity measures should be useful for improving productivity or researching questions with practical value. It is possible to produce highly accurate and sensitive measures, but if these same measures are not useful in helping people in organizations make effective changes that result in productivity improvements, then in our view, the measures have not been successful. Creating successful measures takes time, and especially takes careful consideration of organizations, their goals, and the people who work in them. To help keep measurement development efforts focused on critical success factors, we have defined the four central criteria that follow. These criteria should be considered by anyone whose goal it is to help organizations to produce higher quality goods and services more productively.

These same issues apply to those in research. If an industrial engineer is trying to determine the productivity impact of new technology, all of the rules for measurement effectiveness apply. The social researcher studying the impact and productivity of employee-owned companies must consider these same issues.

Here is a brief statement and explanation of each criterion. Following these is a more complete discussion of each.

Criterion one: quality.–The measure must define and reflect quality of production or services as well as quantity. A measure that assesses only quantity of outputs can lead to reduced productivity.

Criterion two: mission and goals.–The measure must define and assess only outputs and services that are integrated with organizational mission and strategic goals. Measures directed to products and services that are not consistent with mission and goals threaten productivity.

Criterion three: rewards and incentives.–Measures must be integrated with performance incentives, reward systems and practices. Measures that have no important contingencies will not work to improve productivity.

Criterion four: employee involvement.–There must be involvement of organization employees and other direct stakeholders in the definition and construction of productivity measures. When lack of involvement has not resulted in commitment and buy-in, results from the measures are not likely to be received favorably or to have any impact on future productivity.

QUALITY

Quality of goods and services is directly linked to productivity because of the basic truth that "defects are not free" (Deming 1981). It costs an organization to produce flawed, inferior outputs, just as it costs to produce high quality outputs.

Overall Quality

Consider this simple example. The ABC company produces soft drink containers. Current production processes are such that 20% of the containers have defects that keep them from being sold to bottling companies; ABC has to take these defective containers, melt them down, and start production again. Assume that ABC spends $10,000 for each production run of

100,000 containers, for a per-container cost of $.10 (10 cents). But, because only 80,000 containers are usable, the per-container cost for acceptable containers is $.125 (12½ cents) for each salable container. It costs ABC, then, ten cents to produce each defective container as well. In fact, it costs ABC more than this to produce its low quality goods, for ABC has to pay inspectors to find each of the defective containers, and then must pay for the addition reworking costs to melt them down and remanufacture new containers. On top of this, ABC must contend with the fact that, because no inspection process is perfect, some of those defective containers will find their way to bottlers, and even to final customers. The eventual costs to ABC in lost business, replacement of defective goods, even lawsuits, is likely to be well beyond a paltry 10 cents per bottle. Now, consider the effects on productivity if ABC were to change its manufacturing process to achieve higher quality, say a 99.9% defect-free output. Assume further that the costs of higher quality processes are amortized such that each run of 100,000 containers now costs $11,000 versus the prior $10,000. The apparent cost-per-container seems to have risen, from 10 cents each to 11 cents each. But, because ABC gets 99,999 good containers (only one defect per run), the cost of an acceptable container has declined, from 12½ cents to just a hair more than 11 cents. ABC has improved productivity! And, of course, the many associated costs resulting from ABC's prior lower quality production rates will be reduced dramatically as well, thus achieving even greater productivity gains.

This example demonstrates the inevitable relationship between quality and productivity that the American automobile industry, for one, was taught in a rather harsh way by the Japanese (Deming 1981; Hayes 1985; and others). An automobile executive of our acquaintance once told us of his first impressions from a visit to a Japanese auto manufacturer. There he saw cars come off the line in Japan. As each car emerged, into it leaped a driver, who started the motor and drove the auto the short distance to the ship on which it was to be loaded for export. What did he see at his home plant in Detroit? An auto came off the line, after which an inspector entered the car and tried to start it, often unsuccessfully. The non-starting car was then pushed by four other workers off the end of the line to a repair bay where other workers tried to start it. Autos which could not be readily made to run here were pushed further to a repair yard, where a small army of mechanics regularly patrolled among the distressingly large lot of flawed autos! Even if the Japanese were spending somewhat more to produce each auto (which unfortunately for U.S. manufacturers they were not), it was obvious that their higher quality production methods were far more productive, and they could thus spend less per acceptable vehicle.

Clearly, productivity measures must focus on quality. A unit manager who measures only how many minutes of service her unit provides to internal customers, instead of measuring how many minutes of acceptable quality service is provided, will be misled. The focus must be on *production of acceptable quality* versus sheer production.

Quality and the Customer

One very useful definition of quality is "fit for use by the customer." The appeal of this somewhat simplistic definition is that it emphasizes the inevitable role of the customer in arriving at a definition of quality. The products (or services) of an organization, or a unit within an organization, are destined always to be used or consumed by someone—the customers of that unit or organization. The light switches that are made by an automobile parts supplier are provided to the automobile manufacturer (the light switch maker's customer). This automobile manufacturer has set quality specifications for the switch provider, to help the switch provider be sure that each switch made is "fit for use." In this example it is clear that the switch manufacturer had to work closely with the customer in order to understand and define quality standards, for it is the customer's needs that serve as the origin of the quality specifications.

This same relationship between quality specifications and customer expectations permeates all of service and production businesses and organizations. Standards and definitions of quality must take into account the customer's perspective. Often, this means that productivity measurement efforts will entail surveys, or other information collection methods, of both internal and external customers in order to understand quality standards. Productivity improvement needs are not well served when quality definitions are misinformed, or are otherwise inaccurate.

MISSION AND GOALS

The gist of this criterion is extremely simple: Those things that get measured should be important to the goals and mission of an organization. Consider, for example, a store that sells ice cream cones. The mission and goals of this store are, obviously, related to serving customers the ice cream they wish to consume, neatly, in pleasant surroundings, efficiently, and safely. Clearly, then, anything that the store chooses to measure in order to improve productivity must bear directly on these mission and goal dimensions. Measuring customer satisfaction, for instance, or the speed of service, are dimensions that have an obvious and direct bearing on the success of the store in achieving its mission.

In very large and complex organizations, it is sometimes difficult to clarify and maintain a focus on those dimensions that are so obviously and directly related to mission and goals. The authors once were consultants to a large manufacturing company of several thousand employees whose mission was to produce and market certain electronic products to worldwide customers. Like similar organizations, this company had numerous divisions and units, such as marketing, sales, employee relations, research, legal administration, information services, and so forth. In that this was a company particularly oriented to human relations, there was a food services unit within the employee relations division that operated vending machines, snack bars, and a cafeteria for employees. This food services unit was also engaged in a productivity improvement effort with which we were assisting. As would be expected, the food services unit identified dimensions for measurement and improvement that were very similar to those of the ice cream store mentioned in the beginning of this section. That is, customer satisfaction, speed of service, cleanliness, and so forth, were very important considerations. Yet, it was entirely possible that pursuit of improvements in these dimensions could also run counter to the interests of the larger company. Employees might, for example, be more satisfied if the snack bar were to install video games for lunch break entertainment. Such games could clearly, however, interfere with the company's more important goal of having workers return promptly to their work place, and thus would be counterproductive. In their understandable and laudable zeal to satisfy cafeteria patrons, we discovered that food service managers were quite likely to lose sight of the larger company mission and goals relating to efficient production, profits, and so forth. As productivity measurement consultants, we had to make special and laborious efforts to ensure that these unit managers considered higher order company goals as they identified their own unit goals and measurement concerns.

The threat of measuring and improving aspects of operation not essentially vital to overall organization productivity is called the threat of "suboptimization"—optimizing the performance of secondary, or even irrelevant, aspects of operation. The sub-optimization threat is especially valid in today's large and complex organizations where there are literally hundreds of units, each employing many people and consuming increasing amounts of resources. The managers of these units will, quite naturally, tend to focus on their own particular unit's mission and goals, and may, over time, tend to lose sight of *why* their unit exists in the first place. As unit-specific considerations loom larger than company-wide considerations, the threat of sub-optimization looms larger, as well. Sub-optimization threats do not apply only to the unit level of an organization. Particular elements of individual jobs may become, in the eyes of the job incumbent, more important than other job elements, and the larger job goal and its relationship to unit or even company needs may tend to become lost. The authors' recent work in training telephone sales personnel to use newly introduced computers is a good case in point. Many individuals in these jobs became increasingly concerned with the accuracy of inputting data and the speed with which they moved from one screen to another. These concerns overshadowed customer interaction and satisfaction concerns, and sales began to slump. Job operators were sub-optimizing: getting better at performing less important job dimensions.

The implications for productivity measurement are clear. Special care must be taken to ensure that those job, unit, or organization outputs selected for measurement are, in fact, vital to overall productivity. This means that each and every output identified at the job or unit level should be reviewed, and modified as necessary, to be sure it is integrated within the larger organization's mission and goals. The process of reviewing integration is likely, of course, to entail considerable discussion and reflection on mission and goals, and as a result, may lead to differences of opinion and political argument. Almost inevitably, the status quo is threatened, and threats to personal roles and values, real or perceived, are likely to emerge. Those who seek to measure and improve productivity should not let such issues and concerns deter them from the essentail need, however, to carefully investigate the integration of all organization functions and jobs with the larger mission and goals.

REWARDS AND INCENTIVES

"What's in it for me?" This query, albeit somewhat cynically abrupt, quite neatly sums up the third productivity measure criterion: There must be some consequence for achieving positive results on productivity measures (Perry 1988). This criterion is perhaps easiest to relate to in its negative expression. If there were absolutely no perceived reason for performance—if it made no difference whatsoever whether performance was at, above, or below a measurable standard—then it is easy to understand that the performer would be unlikely to pay any attention to the measurement data. Measures must make a difference in the welfare of the person or unit being measured, or the measures will have virtually no attention paid to them.

The differences that measures must make can, of course, vary widely. And, the value framework of the persons being measured must be considered. The rewards and incentives attached to productivity measures can be as tangible as salary increases and bonuses, or as intangible as recognition and public praise. But, whatever the rewards or incentives, they must be perceived as important to those whose performance is being measured. We know of organizations that have carefully administered programs that provide regular monthly recognition for measured productivity increases, posting pictures of high performers in the employee cafeteria, and printing articles about them and their achievements in the local newspaper. Other organizations provide cash awards and gifts, such as wristwatches or small appliances. And yet other organizations tie productivity measures to promotions and salary increases. In these organizations, measured productivity is seen as important, and measured performance makes a difference that matters to people. As a result, the measurement process has caught hold.

At the other end of the spectrum, we have worked with organizations where there is only "lip service" paid to productivity measures. In one large company, we worked for several years to help install productivity measures in each of the company's hundreds of units. The chairman of the board appointed a board level "czar" of productivity, who wrote articles and issued many mandates—mandates that carried the board chair's signature. Yet despite all the hoopla and considerable expense for support materials and measurement training, virtually no units ever made use of productivity measures in their unit planning and operation. Managers in this company soon discovered that having and using unit productivity measures really made little difference in the overall scheme of things. Managers who implemented no measures at all seemed to be successful, gaining promotions and adding staff and receiving bonuses. Other managers who installed and used measures sometimes received no such rewards. The attitude soon spread throughout the cultural network that the much touted measurement system was not really important after all, and the productivity measurement movement in this organization died a relatively quick death. Today, business goes on as usual, and productivity measures are almost nowhere to be seen.

Tying productivity measurement into the reward and incentive system of an organization is especially critical early in a productivity measurement effort. Eventually, as measures are used and relied upon to make planning and operating decisions, they become self-rewarding and tend to perpetuate themselves. Consider, for example (and if you can remember), your own behavior when first you began to use a personal checking account. Typically, you would have to consciously drive yourself to record checks written, and reconcile monthly bank statements. As you learned the consequences of failing to use any measurement information (by bouncing checks and paying overdraft charges), chances are you learned to maintain at least some sort of measurement system, and you paid attention to the feedback provided both from your personal check register and the bank's regular statements. As people in an organization are introduced to measuring and using the results of productivity performance, they will probably require very visible and direct incentives for adopting these new behavior patterns (Landy et al. 1983). Over time, however, if measures do really make a difference, they will become a part of the regular job behavior patterns.

Meeting the criterion of consequence demands a commitment from the highest levels of management in the organization. If the reward and incentive system is not performance-based, then change in the reward/incentive system and culture must precede a productivity measurement effort (Perry 1988). In organizations, for example, where people can get promotions, earn salary increases, or otherwise meet their status and recognition needs whether they perform well on the job or not, productivity measurement efforts will be futile. For these reasons, those who wish to lead and support productivity measurement programs will have to first gain an understanding of how an organization works, its culture, and especially how it distributes reward, recognition, and incentive.

EMPLOYEE INVOLVEMENT

The final criterion of the four that successful productivity measures must meet relates not to what is measured, but how decisions regarding what, when, and how to measure get made. Deciding to adopt productivity measurement systems requires a multitude of decisions ranging over a variety of dimensions, including who will do the measuring, when measures will be done, to whom reports will be made, and so forth, to name just a few. (Chapters 7 and 8 discuss these processes in detail.)

You will recall that the authors have defined the success of productivity measurement as the extent to which productivity measurement data are used to impact and improve productivity. Such success depends in large part on the feelings of employees about the measurement effort (Puckett 1985). If such feelings are positive, seeing the system as helpful, fair, open, honest, consequential, important, and so forth, then the likelihood of employees actually using measures dramatically increases. On the other hand, if the measurement effort is seen as partial, biased, unimportant, ill-conceived, or an effort by management to punish or exploit employees and squeeze them unfairly for unendingly greater amounts of work, then the effort is almost sure to be sabotaged. In addition, any organizational performance consultant with even a little experience knows that the capacity of employees to sabotage or "end run" even the best designed system is infinite!

The most practical approach to facilitating adoption and promoting usage is involvement. Employees should be visibly and tangibly involved in the productivity measurement planning process from the very start (Shetty and Buehler 1985). Such involvement not only breeds adoption, it is smart business. When looking for information and trying to make progress, it is only smart to get the best information available—get the best expertise you can. If top management is doing its proper job of delegating authority, then the people most knowledgeable about how jobs really work are the job performers themselves. To not involve job holders in measurement planning and productivity improvement is to ignore the greatest experts. As consultants, we are sometimes asked by companies and organizations seeking assistance: "Do you know any productivity experts?" Our seemingly flip but very honest response is "Yes—they already work for you!" Then, we can proceed to explain our need to involve employees very thoroughly and closely in all steps in the productivity measurement planning process.[1]

Involvement of employees in productivity measurement planning and implementation yields a number of benefits, each helping to assure a useful measurement effort. As noted above, job holders themselves are most knowledgeable about the details of jobs, and are thus best able to conduct the sort of analysis that leads to the identification of critical work dimensions and measures. The process of involvement, especially when it is perceived as open and honest, leads to "buy-in" and commitment. Employees are much more likely to use, and much less likely to sabotage, a system that they themselves have helped to build.

Involvement also achieves the necessary goal of awareness and understanding of productivity measurement purposes and procedures in the organization. It is vitally important that all those employees involved in and potentially impacted by the measurement program be fully aware of it. Nothing will breed suspicion and feed rumors more quickly than ignorance and misinformation. Employees who have been involved from the beginning in reviewing plans, making suggestions, drafting measures and so forth, will be informed as to the means and ends of the productivity measurement effort. The final chapter of this book returns to the topic of employee involvement as it outlines and discusses methods that organizations can use to promote, build, and operate successful measurement programs.

This criterion means that management is still essential to productivity measurement/improvement. Ultimately, management must allocate time, money and support for these efforts. Yet, if it is only a management effort, it will be minimally effective.

SUMMARY

In this chapter we have listed and discussed four essential criteria that successful productivity measures should meet. As we noted at the beginning of the chapter, measures must first be accurate. That is, measures should not be so sloppy and unreliable as to provide misinformation about important productivity dimensions. The accuracy of a measure is clearly important, but it is also basically only a technical issue. Accuracy is relatively easy to achieve, and at most is a matter of obtaining technical expertise. The accuracy of a measure, however, says little about whether that measure will be used effectively to monitor and improve operations to impact productivity. Further, a measure could be highly accurate, but could be accurately measuring something that has little or no bearing on true productivity. Thus, in this chapter we have posed four criteria that go beyond accuracy. First and foremost, a measure must include dimensions of quality, because improvements in quality will lead inexorably to improved productivity. Secondly, a measure must assess performance that is central to the success of the organization, and so must be integrated with the mission of the organization. The final two criteria relate more to the political context of the organization, and bear heavily on whether the people within an organization will adopt and embrace measures. Thus, the third criterion directed that a measure must be integrated with the organization's formal and informal reward and recognition system. The final and fourth criterion calls for the involvement of employees, noting that measures that are not derived through a participatory process are very likely doomed to fail.

The remaining chapters of this book will deal in more detail with these four criteria as we we proceed to discuss methods and "how to" approaches for creating useful measures and implementing successful measurement programs.

NOTE

1. For guidance and help on employee involvement, see Moore 1987.

4

Outputs in Productivity Measurement

In the preceding chapters, we have laid out a conceptual framework and conceptual guidelines for productivity measurement activities which are critical for success in any attempt at productivity measurement and improvement. The next three chapters will introduce you to the specific steps necessary to establish productivity indices for an organization, a unit, or for an individual performer.

In this chapter, you will be introduced to the specific steps to determine outputs for inclusion in a productivity measurement index. Initially, outputs of any organization, unit, or job seem evident. However, outputs are often not clearly understood nor correctly defined so that they can be measured. We first discuss the concept of "output," drawing on examples from many different settings. Following this, we present the important concept of levels of output, showing how output measurement often must be based on a careful analysis of production procedures. The chapter includes a discussion of outputs in white collar and other "hard to measure" settings. As American industry moves increasingly toward a service economy, such settings are more commonplace.

The chapter closes with a presentation of some of the special considerations and criteria that researchers, managers, and others who aim to measure productivity should keep in mind when working to measure outputs.

OUTPUTS DEFINED

Outputs, in their simplest form, are "the goods and services produced" by any individual, unit, or organization (Riggs and Felix 1983). Thus, in a generic productivity ratio, the output (numerator) is:

$$\text{Productivity} = \frac{\text{goods and services produced (outputs)}}{\text{inputs}}$$

However, in the face of increased worldwide competition and a consistent emphasis on quality, we would argue that a better definition for outputs would be: "the number of goods and services produced that are usable, salable and of acceptable quality.'' Many organizations still operate with the notion that productivity is a raw count of goods and services produced. In Chapter 3, we illustrated how quality and productivity are vitally linked. We must include this concept in the definition of outputs.

This link is rather easy to illustrate. Suppose that, last month, a baker was able to produce 20 coffee cakes an hour. This month, he produces 22 coffee cakes of equal quality per hour. His productivity has increased 10%. Also, if 20 coffee cakes were produced per hour last month and 20 coffee cakes of higher quality are produced per hour this month, productivity has also risen, although the measurement of the increase may be more difficult to make. Another baker making 20 quality coffee cakes per hour last month may make 22 per hour this month. But, if 2 of these cakes are defective, so that he still makes only 20 quality coffee cakes, productivity has actually gone down due to increased material and utility costs to produce the same 20 quality cakes. The concept of measuring quality and quantity when establishing outputs must be extended to any goods and services produced.

Kinds of Output Measures

Having defined outputs as a unique measure of quantity and quality of goods and services produced, we turn to a framework for determining output measures in a diversity of organizations and situations. The first step is to decide the level of the measurement system. Until that decision is made, output measures cannot be accurately determined. Outputs can generally be measured at two general levels:

- the final products or services of an entire organization, and
- the intermediate outputs in an organization, which may or may not become part of the final products or services.

Referring again to the carwash example in an earlier chapter, we note that the final output is ''a washed and waxed car.'' An intermediate output, however, is the result of the washing operation: ''a washed car ready for waxing.'' In this setting, measurement could be aimed at the final output, or at the intermediate output, or both.

Every organization, whether in manufacturing or service, has one or more final outputs. These are the goods and services that ''exit'' the business so that they can be purchased by other individuals or organizations. Typically, any business has many intermediate outputs; these are all the interim goods and services that must be produced so that they can be incorporated into, or support the development and sale of, the final product.

Consider the organizational output of a manufacturer of home cleaning equipment. The output measure at the final output level for this manufacturer might be the number of quality, salable cleaning units produced.

Consider now the definition and measurement of outputs at the intermediate level. The manufacturer making carpet and floor cleaning equipment has numerous intermediate outputs. The company's electric motor assembly unit produces a quantity of usable motors each day. That output can and should be measured. The plastic injection unit makes a number of vacuum cannister units to certain specifications each day. That output should be measured. The paint department paints some number of sweeper units per day. That output should be measured. There are other critical outputs that are essential for the production of the final organizational output, and thus they should be considered for measurement.

Intermediate outputs can also be defined and measured at even greater levels of specificity. For instance, in the motor assembly unit, one could measure the output of the machine that winds the electrical coil, the person who assembles the motor housing, the person who attaches the wiring harness, and finally the person and machine that does the quality check for motor performance. All of these outputs are intermediate outputs of the motor assembly department, and all are essential for creating a quality intermediate output (the electric motor) in sufficient quantity for the organization to then use to manufacture its final output, the carpet cleaning machine.

Outputs can and should be measured at various levels in most organizations. Only when an organization is relatively small, simple, and has a homogeneous output is a single output measure sufficient. An example of such an organization with a homogeneous output is an ice making company. Measuring the quantity and quality of ice produced might be an adequate measure. However, most organizations have complex outputs, requiring a number of output measures to adequately determine and modify productivity. An example of such an organization would be a plastics manufacturing plant. This plant may have multiple machines and systems producing a variety of plastic parts. These might range from typewriter keys to drinking cups. In this case, distinct measurement systems may be needed to track the productivity of each operation. Further, it may be useful to track productivity at finer levels within sub-divisions, such as the materials handling department, the injection department, the inventory department, the shipping department, and so forth.

By segmenting the output measures in complex organizations, you measure not only the "out the door" outputs, but the many goods and services consumed internally: those needed to produce the "out the door" products. Many productivity gains have been made by measuring the internally consumed goods and services in an organization. A good productivity record for finished products can be made even better by attention to efficiency throughout the organization.

While many manufacturing organizations do not measure intermediate outputs, almost all collect substantial amounts of data on their final outputs, including customer satisfaction data. Automobile companies, for example, measure not only rate of production, quality, quantity, and so forth; they also spend considerable resources tracking customer satisfaction with their products through elaborate post-sale surveys. This same degree of attention to measuring final "products" is not, however, typical of service organizations in either the private or public sector.

More than likely, the relative lack of measurement in the service sector is attributable to the fact that a service produces no tangible product, and thus measurement appears to be more difficult. It is hard to measure, so goes the common wisdom, what you cannot see, touch, or feel. Yet, as any person who has received either very good or very poor service can tell you, service has a very noticeable effect. Our contention is a simple one: service organizations exist to make a difference; making a difference is, in fact, what a service organization is all about. Thus, the nature and the degree of difference a service organization provides is highly measurable, and ought to be measured as well.[1]

The importance of measurement in service organizations cannot be overemphasized. The service business is highly labor intensive and characterized by relatively low margins. Further, it is extremely competitive, as new entrepreneurs can (and do) venture into competition with almost no capital investment. Competitive advantage is gained through consistent achievement of high levels of customer satisfaction. Identifying customer expectations, assessing efforts to meet these expectations, and monitoring service activities to maintain satisfaction requires pervasive and systematic measurement. Managers, researchers, and others who are involved in service organizations must become proficient in the measurement of service results, an already rich and growing arena of endeavor.

As is true in the production business field, measurement of service outputs should be conducted at the intermediate as well as the final level.

A home cleaning service may have the mission of providing quality home cleaning services in a highly competitive market while earning a fair return on invested company dollars and providing meaningful employment for its workers. Given that mission, final output measures are not that difficult to determine. Clearly, one output measure might be the number of homes cleaned in a week. However, the word "quality" in the mission statement must be factored in. A better measure would be the number of homes cleaned per week that are noted "highly satisfactory" (via a telephone follow-up) by customers. If the company provided a satisfaction guaranteed offer, the output might be the number of homes cleaned during the week minus the number of return cleanings required to satisfy customers.

At the intermediate level, home cleaning outputs could be measured on a "per crew" basis. The telemarketing department of the company might be measured on the number of sales made per month. The supervisor of cleaning crews might be measured on the number of home inspections made per month following home cleaning by a crew. Each of these are essential elements for achieving the mission of the organization. Each element could also cost the company lost productivity if it failed to perform its separate task effectively and efficiently.

A very powerful tool used in determining outputs at many levels in an organization is called organizational mapping (Rummler 1982b). This process, a rather simple procedure, traces the use of raw materials, labor, and processes in an organization. Figures 4.1 and 4.2 provide examples of functional maps which display major functional units and depict (by arrows) their dependencies. The arrows in the map show that one function provides an input to another function. Figure 4.1 shows functions for an entire organization, while Figure 4.2 demonstrates a functional mapping of a unit within an organization. At each point in the process, it is possible to determine outputs from one individual/unit. These often become the inputs for the next process. This new unit's outputs become the inputs for another process. This can be traced throughout the organization until the final product is out the door. Organizational mapping is an easy and powerful way to identify outputs at almost any point in the organization.

OUTPUT MEASURES FOR HARD-TO-MEASURE JOBS

Productivity measurement systems have been closely associated with time and motion studies in manufacturing organizations. Often, hourly workers in the manufacturing environment have felt the pressures of productivity measurement/improvement. Management, in the same company, has often been unaccountable for specific productivity gains. In most cases, little measuring of management productivity is done. "It can't be done," is the usual argument.

While it is admittedly difficult to define and operationalize the outputs of management functions, it is not impossible. To define and measure management (and other "white collar") outputs is advisable from a number of perspectives (Lehrer 1983). Our experience consistently reveals that management uses the measurement difficulty argument as a "smoke screen" behind which to hide to avoid accountability. Clearly, then, a visible and

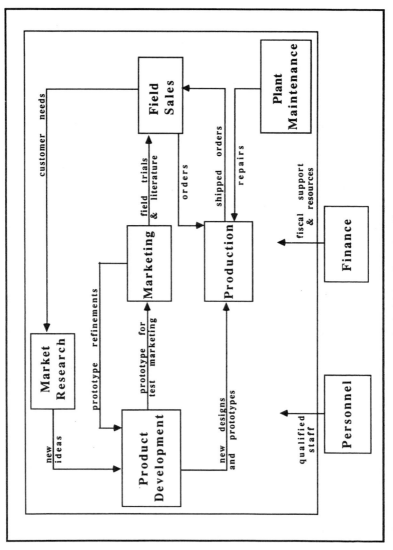

Figure 4.1. Functional Map for a Hypothetical Manufacturing Company

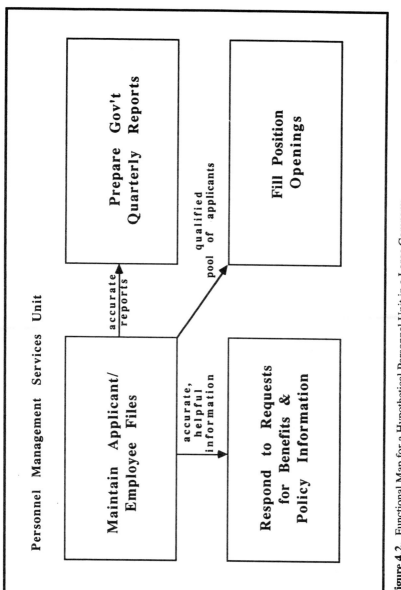

Personnel Management Services Unit

Prepare Gov't Quarterly Reports

Fill Position Openings

Maintain Applicant/ Employee Files

Respond to Requests for Benefits & Policy Information

accurate reports

qualified pool of applicants

accurate, helpful information

Figure 4.2. Functional Map for a Hypothetical Personnel Unit in a Large Company

committed effort to measure and account for management performance strengthens an overall measurement effort and reduces "we-they" fractiousness. An additional reason for identifying management outputs and targeting them for measurement is because of the often observed truism that: "What gets measured, gets done."

The main reason for measuring outputs of white collar functions, however, is to assess and improve productivity. While one can certainly argue reasonably that many large businesses are bloated with mid-level managers, it is also clear that a modern, complex bureaucratic organization requires a variety of functions and internal "services," such as legal affairs, personnel, training, employee assistance, and so forth. It is also clear that each functional unit must do its job, and do it well, for the overall operation to succeed. And this is where measurement of "hard to measure" functions applies.

Consider, for example, a fast food restaurant. In a typical fast food restaurant, you will find one store manager and usually two to four assistant managers. What is their purpose in the store and what productivity should they be held accountable for? One assistant manager is usually responsible for employee selection and hiring. That manager makes a significant contribution to store productivity when a large pool of potential employees is maintained and when interviewing and selection procedures are effective in hiring high-level performers who stay with the store for more than two months. It can be demonstrated that both of these job outputs can make significant impacts on improved customer service, reduced training costs, reduced paperwork, and reduced store costs because of fewer mistakes in ordering. It is possible to measure the applicant pool maintained and the hiring/selection record of the assistant manager. As will be shown in the next chapter, the costs of creating those outputs are also measurable.

A supervisory position in a manufacturing plant may seem to have few measurable job outputs. That, however, is not the case. In an effort to provide consumers with quality products at competitive prices, the supervisor must do many things, many of which are readily measurable. The number of employee grievances can be traced. The human resources manager at an automotive parts manufacturing plant estimated that employee grievances that go to arbitration cost the company $5000 each. A supervisor able to solve employee problems at the shop level may save thousands of dollars a year in costs. Typically, those costs must either be added to the price consumers pay or be subtracted from company profits. Supervisors should also be responsible for the training of their reporting employees. If training directly targets quality production, the quality output of one supervisor can be measured and compared to other supervisors.

For upper level management, output measures are definable if one takes the time to carefully analyze the job outputs and how they work to deliver goods and services to paying consumers. Often, upper level management is responsible for company communication. Content and quality analysis of communication products can be measured, and employees can be asked if they feel adequately informed.

Upper level managers also conduct numerous meetings. Productive meetings are those that have prepared agendas focusing on issues that only those in the meeting can decide/help with, and are kept on target and moving. It is possible to measure if managers are conducting productive meetings. It is also possible to calculate the company cost for a two hour meeting for a half dozen managers each being paid $25 an hour. Likewise, the speed with which decisions are made and the number of approval steps needed to get decisions made are not only big productivity factors, but can be readily measured. The potential gains in productivity are enormous at the upper levels of management as well.

We would suggest that companies take seriously the opportunity to measure and improve the productivity of hard-to-measure jobs. If the job contributes to meeting consumers' needs directly, or helps those who meet the needs of consumers, then it has measurable outputs. If it does not do the above, then of course it should be eliminated from the company.

SPECIAL CONSIDERATIONS FOR OUTPUT MEASURES

There are a number of criteria that measured outputs must meet if they are to be incorporated successfully into effective productivity measurement efforts. Some of these have already been noted in the previous chapters, and others will be revisited in the closing two chapters which discuss approaches to building effective measurement procedures. Finally, the output measures must meet the general measurement criteria discussed in Chapter 3, as these apply to virtually any measurement effort. Since our topic has been constrained to output measurement, we list and briefly discuss here the major criteria that impinge specifically on output measurement.

1. Outputs Must Be Important and Integrated with the Organization Mission

The rule of thumb here is that we should count (measure) only that which is important. Some outputs clearly count more than others. In a bakery, for example, we might identify "number of products per baked-goods category (doughnuts, coffee cakes, and so forth)" as an important output, since we would certainly want to meet customer demands for each category. On the other hand, the equally measurable output "number of baked products per display tray" would be far less important. Meeting customer demands for certain kinds of products is very central to the baker's mission, and variations in this output would drastically affect the accomplishment of the mission. Variations in the number of doughnuts per tray, however (as long as there were enough total doughnuts) could have little, if any, such impact on mission achievement.

Of the many possible outputs that might be identified for any given organization, only a few will yield sufficiently potent measurement information on which critical productivity decisions can be made. The trick for applied researchers and managers in organizations is to identify those few outputs worth measuring.

2. Criteria on Which Outputs Are Measured Must Respond to "Customer" Expectations

We have, in many instances, stressed the importance of quality in the productivity formula. Quality increases create productivity gains, since rework, customer returns, and so forth, are automatically reduced. But it must be remembered that quality is a relative quantity; quality, like beauty and the beholder, is in the eyes of the customer. In fact, a very workable definition of quality is: "Fit for use by the customer."

If something is not deemed acceptable by customers, then regardless of how good it otherwise is, it fails the quality test. Assume, for example, that we decide to open a pizza shop. Believing strongly in good nutrition, we load our pizzas with whole wheat flour, oat bran, and brewers yeast. We also carefully assess the quality of our pizzas against the very strongest criteria we have developed. According to our measures, we produce only the highest quality pizzas. We also go out of business. Our pizzas fail the customer satisfaction test, because they fail to measure up to the criteria that customers require.

The electric motors produced by the motor unit in the carpet cleaner company must be acceptable to the assembly division; the market analyses produced by market research must not only be accurate, they must be readable and acceptable to the product development division, and so on. In business and service, things are made and done for either internal or external customers. Quality criteria must reflect and respond to these customer's needs and expectations.

3. There Must Be a "Buy In" to Outputs and Their Measurement

This criterion is not truly a characteristic of outputs themselves, but rather is acquired through the process by which outputs are identified and selected for measurement. Later chapters in this book will discuss this topic in considerably more detail, as it is extremely important. We put it here as a reminder, to stress its importance.

In almost any setting, productivity measurement efforts will be accompanied by varying degrees of resistance among staff. They may perceive the efforts as threatening, and may attempt to sabotage the measurement system. Human beings in organizations seem to display an innate and endless capacity to foil virtually any and all management control schemes. Productivity measurement is no exception.

Involvement is not only a practical issue. People whose efforts are going to be measured have an ethical right to at least be made aware of the measurement system and criteria, and by all rules of fairness and humane treatment should have a voice in determining what about their work gets measured, how it is measured, and who will measure it. Nothing will bring an otherwise well-intentioned and sophisticated measurement system crashing down around the researcher's or manager's ears more quickly than a violation of this tenet.

4. Those Employees Whose Outputs Are Measured Must Have Control Over the Outputs

When productivity results are controlled by anyone outside the producing unit, there is a lack of ownership for productivity improvement.

We recently worked with a client in a telemarketing business who relied on a new, complex, centralized computer system. Early in the start up, it was apparent that several productivity issues were beyond the control of the job performers in this company. One of these variables had to do with electrical power. The nerve center was located in an area of explosive residential and commercial growth. The local power company had not been able to provide quality electrical services to the entire area, which experienced a high incidence of power brownouts and complete blackouts. Since performers were completely dependent on electric service for computer operations, productivity suffered. In this case, the performers were not completely in control of a major factor affecting their productivity. Thus, our measurement scheme had to factor in and adjust for frequent "down time" periods.

Similar examples exist within many organizations. A truck assembly company could produce far more quality trucks at the end of the line if purchasing had the proper quantity and quality of parts for assembly. Purchasing could have the proper quantity and quality parts if assembly kept them informed of truck orders and parts inventory. This is a further argument for productivity measurement that looks at overall organizational effectiveness, not just at a single unit level or performer's productivity. An organization that depends on the outputs of one unit for inputs to a second unit (as virtually all organizations do), must build productivity measurement systems that hold any one unit accountable for that which it controls. Other measures are clearly useful, but may demonstrate other units with productivity problems and not the unit being measured.

DEFINING CRITERIA FOR MEASUREMENT

Measurement criteria specify the particular attributes and characteristics of the output that are deemed to be most important. If, in the example of a bakery, we defined a key output as "doughnuts," we would then have to specify what about the doughnuts ought to be measured: their weight? flavor? texture? number? size? fluffiness? appearance? shape? To enable measurement, of course, these defining attributes would have to be further operationalized, for example: "weight when at room temperature from 1.0 to 1.3 ounces," or "do not crumble when broken."

Criteria for measurement should, of course, derive directly from and respond to the expectations and needs of customers. And, criteria should be thoroughly reviewed by those who are responsible for producing outputs to be sure that they are reasonable and fair.

Listed below, in Table 4.1 are categories of criteria that typically are of interest to both internal and external customers.

TECHNIQUES FOR MEASURING OUTPUTS

There are many methods that can be used to measure outputs. Selection and design of methods depends primarily, of course, on the nature of the output to be measured and the criteria deemed important. (Readers are reminded that Chapter 2 discusses guidelines for measurement in general, and provides steps and procedures for developing measures.)

In general, there are two types of measures that are typically applied to outputs. The first are direct measures of the overt characteristics of the

Table 4.1

Common Kinds of Criteria for Measurement Outputs

- Accuracy: within X% of Y, less than 5% variation, and so forth.
- Timeliness: when done, not later than, within X period, before, and so forth.
- Historical standards: more than before, less than X period, same as last year, and so forth.
- Comparative standards: more than X, less than Y, equal to Z's performance, larger than a bread box, and so forth.
- Engineering specifications: specific length, size, shape, ingredient, makeup, and so forth.
- Manner of performance: consistency, frequency, reliability, variation, and so forth.
- Quantity: number of pieces, sets, groups, elements, and so forth.
- Physical characteristics: size, weight, height, length, thickness, shape, and so forth.
- Consumer behaviors: satisfaction, agreement, acceptance, endorsement, and so forth.
- Aesthetic ratings: beauty, appearance, compatibility, prominence, and so forth.
- Sensory attributes: smell, taste, touch, feel, hue, texture, and so forth.
- Conditions for performance: when used by X, will . . .; or, when rated by Y, will . . .; or, when observed by C, will . . .; or, when weighed on a carat scale will . . . .
- Cost performance: cheaper than, equal to, no more than, and so forth.
- Completeness: all parts done, all elements present, 80% of total, and so forth.
- Positive standards: increased, larger than, more than, equal to, and so forth.
- Negative standards: less than, lower than, decreased by, fewer than X defects, and so forth.
- Zero standards: absolute levels of tolerances, no deviation, perfect, absence of complaints, and so forth.

output. These are the observable attributes that are displayed by the output when it is complete, or during stages of its development or production.

For tangible products, these overt characteristics are the physical attributes or operating performance of the product. A finished carpet cleaner, for example, might be measured according to (1) the decibels of noise created by the motor, (2) freedom of defects in fit and finish, and (3) foot pounds of suction generated at the end of the cleaning hose. Or, for another example, a doughnut might be measured according to (1) its weight in grams, (2) freedom from flaws in appearance, and (3) internal temperature on removal from the oven.

In the case of services, overt characteristics describe the timeliness, completeness, or other attributes of the service. An automobile oil change shop in our town, for example, makes a manager complete a checklist to be sure that each element of service (radiator check, oil refill, and so forth) are, in fact, delivered and complete. The manager also checks to see whether the service was completed in the time allotted. A telemarketing operation uses a computer to measure the amount of time elapsed prior to answering a call, and calculates the number of calls "on hold," duration on hold, and abandonment rate of calls on hold, all significant outputs of the telemarketing process. A pizza delivery operation checks to see whether deliveries were completed, whether the pies arrived undamaged, whether the pies matched orders, and whether pies arrived within the allotted time.

The second major type of measure represents the impact of the presenting attributes of the output (product or service) by gauging the reactions and opinions of the consumer of the output. The pizza shop might also, for example, measure the degree of satisfaction of the customer with (a) the pizza's flavor, appearance, taste, and so forth, (b) the timeliness of delivery, and (c) the demeanor and professional appearance of the deliveryperson.

Customer reactions and opinions are based, of course, on the presenting attributes of the output. Presumably, the pizza customer feels satisfaction if the order is correct, is delivered on time, tastes good, is presented courteously, and so forth. If all the measured attributes are present and meet specified criteria, yet customers report major dissatisfaction, then there must be some "missing" attribute that has evaded measurement attention. Perhaps customers also want pizza delivered in a sturdy box, or have some other expectation.

One major advantage of measuring customer satisfaction is that it provides an opportunity to (1) validate existing quality criteria, and (2) to identify emerging and shifting expectations so that new criteria can be specified and incorporated into production procedures. A further advantage is that measurement of customer reactions demonstrates customer concern and earns customer regard and loyalty.

If measurement of customer reactions provides such significant advantages, one might ask, then why bother with measuring direct attributes of the output? The answer is partially related to cost. Surveying customers reactions to goods and services is very costly. It is usually much less costly to assess the direct attributes of the service or product, as such measures can typically be readily made as a part of the final production or service delivery process. A second, and important, reason to measure outputs directly is that such measurement permits defective outputs to be held back (and reworked, if possible) before they reach the customer, thus avoiding damage to customer relations.

In the category of direct measures, there are many techniques available. They include such measures as:

- keeping records of rates, returns, volume, frequency, arrivals, departures, and so on.
- inspecting for defects, flaws, irregularities, errors, and so on
- direct gauging of heat, size, weight, firmness, resistance, clarity, and so on
- trials of usage, wear, durability, strength, and so on

- using judges for taste, appearance, comparisons, readability, and so on
- analysis of traces, residues, scraps, and so on

In the category of collecting customer opinion, there are fewer options. Typical procedures include interviews by telephone or in person, telephone or written surveys, group interviews, and self-mail detachable cards and small survey forms. Less direct, but nonetheless useful, measures of customer satisfaction can be derived from analysis of returns, complaints, repeat business, and so forth.

SOME TYPICAL OUTPUTS

Table 4.2 lists some measurable outputs as they might be typically defined for a number of job roles and functions. None of these, of course, are likely to be suitable "as is" for any given application; we offer them so that they may help readers define measurable outputs for jobs and functions in their own applications.

DISCUSSION OF THE SAMPLE OUTPUTS

Perhaps the most noticeable characteristic of the outputs listed is that none of them totally defines the outputs (results) of any job or organizational function. This "reduction" is an inevitable phenomenon of measurement; when we claim to measure something, we actually only measure something about that something.

This inevitable reduction of the meaning of a function's result needs discussion. Consider, for example, the output listed for the "Cost Estimator" in Table 4.2: "Number of reports completed on time." Clearly, a cost estimator's job entails production of reports, and in fact these reports are a major and tangible job output. Further, a cost estimator who consistently produces more reports than any other cost estimator is probably more productive. But there are other dimensions of performance that matter. A cost estimator might, for instance, file a great number of reports, yet in haste to look good on the "number measure," might file incomplete and error-ridden reports. Or, in a similarly misguided effort to raise production, estimators might treat customers brusquely and perfunctorily in order to complete their reports.

People will inevitably work toward measures, believing that what gets counted, must count. This tendency is partially a productive force, because

Table 4.2
Some Typical Outputs

Accountant	Number of accurate verifications of financial reports for customers
Actor	Number of roles played
Automotive mechanic	Proportion of all repairs that are completed without complaint or return
Bank teller	Number of deposits processed without errors
Building custodian	Square feet of area cleaned nightly that meet inspection criteria
Cashier	Proportion of customers served who receive correct change
Chemist	Number of research reports completed on schedule
Childcare worker	Number of children cared for without parent complaint
Computer programmer	Proportion of all programs designed that are accepted by customers
Construction & building inspector	Number of inspections accurately conducted per week
Cook	Proportion of orders filled accurately and on time
Cost estimator	Number of reports completed on time
Designer	Number of designs accepted by customers
Employment interviewer	Number of interview reports accurately completed
Faculty	Number of doctoral students graduated per year
Financial manager	Proportion of clients who are ''fully satisfied'' with services received
Lawyer	Proportion of satisfied clients
Pilot	Proportion of flights flown within incident requiring filing of FAA Incident Form
Priest	Number of hospital visitors trained

it drives performance toward goals. Yet, if performance works exaggeratedly toward some measured goals at the expense of other important goals, then productivity can suffer. The world witnessed a very dramatic and tragic example of this tendency when the *Challenger* space shuttle exploded; investigation of the crash revealed that the pressure to perform on time (a heavily measured dimension) probably overrode a number of quality and safety concerns. In our own experience with a telemarketing operation, when the number of calls answered per hour was accentuated by measurement, call handlers tended to treat customers too briskly and brusquely, and overall sales declined. When other measures (proportion of calls converted to a sale) were highlighted, the problem was resolved.

Because no single measure is ever likely to represent enough of what is important about a job or function, multiple measures are recommended.

We urge researchers and managers to employ "families" of measures, to be sure that no single measure is allowed to distort the result of a job. The cost estimator, for example, could be measured on (1) number of reports filed, (2) freedom of reports from error, incompleteness, and so forth and (3) satisfaction of customers with the cost estimator's performance. Such families of measures tend to provide balance, and afford more holistic views of job results. We return to this notion in Chapter 6, especially where multi-factor measures are discussed.

SUMMARY

In this chapter we have defined outputs at two levels. Final outputs are "the useable, salable, acceptable quality goods and services produced" by the organization. Intermediate outputs are those goods and services produced by units and sub-units which are, in turn, provided to other units or sub-units. We have argued that measuring only the goods and services produced, without paying attention to the "quality" factor, ignores the major gain to be made in productivity measurement/improvement. We have stressed the important role of customer expectations in defining quality criteria.

We have suggested that outputs should be measured at various levels in the organization. Outputs can be measured for the organization as a whole, for units within an organization and for individual workers and machines. Many goods-producing organizations have some measure of organizational outputs. The same is not always true in service industries, and typically greater efforts to define outputs and their criteria are needed.

We have included numerous examples of output measures for various organizations, both service and manufacturing. This should provide a framework for the reader to begin doing output analyses for jobs and organizations with which they are familiar.

And finally, we have listed some special considerations for implementing productivity measurement systems.

In the next chapter, we will fill in the input side of the productivity measurement system.

NOTE

1. It is in the expanding arena of service businesses that productivity measurement overlaps very noticeably with the discipline of program evaluation, for which there is abundant literature. See the References for additional readings on this topic.

5

Measuring Inputs

In the previous chapter, we dealt with the topic of measuring outputs. In this chapter, we move to the second half of the productivity equation: inputs. When outputs are measured, then production can be gauged, reflecting the amount, rate, characteristics, or other dimensions of the flow of goods and services created by an organization. Until the costs of production are considered, however, true productivity cannot be determined.

Typically, an organization tends to concentrate its attention and measurement efforts on outputs. If an organization is going to measure anything, chances are it will measure outputs. This is true for a number of reasons, almost all stemming from the common culture and popular wisdom that says that "results" are everything. An organization exists to move products and services "out the door" and thus employees from top to bottom in the organization are concerned with what they see as getting the job done: producing. The end result is that at worst, input measurement tends to get ignored or, at best, it gets the short shrift.

Inputs are equally important to the productivity measurement effort. If production increases, yet the consumption of resources increases more quickly, then true productivity suffers. The recent decline of a number of American industries, especially the automobile business, represents a painful example of this truth. As labor and energy costs in America have risen, productivity has declined, and foreign competitors have gained market shares. When managers and organization researchers help focus attention on inputs, and help clarify and track the consumption of resources, greater efficiencies can be obtained, and innovative cost-saving efforts can be assessed.

In this chapter, we first define and discuss the major categories of inputs that should be measured. A presentation and discussion of considerations and guidelines for input measurement follows this section. Next, we provide some steps and suggestions on how to measure inputs. This chapter closes with a listing of numerous examples of input measures.

INPUTS DEFINED

Inputs are the resources consumed in producing the goods and services of an organization. Consider, for example, a doughnut shop that produces a variety of doughnuts for sale to customers. The very obvious inputs in this example are such things as flour, sugar, other ingredients, ovens, recipes, and all of the other resources needed to make doughnuts. Then, of course, there are the people needed to bake and sell the doughnuts, the electricity to heat the ovens, and the shop itself, among other resources. Finally, less directly involved inputs might be identified such as the costs of advertising and marketing, insurance, janitorial services to clean up the shop after hours, and so forth.

We have typically grouped inputs into five major categories: personnel, capital, energy, materials, and services (sometimes called "indirect labor" costs). We will proceed to discuss each of these in more detail in the following section, but first let us return to the doughnut shop example to characterize each catgory further. Personnel might include the bakers and retail counter staff; energy includes the electricity to heat the ovens and light the shop and display cases; materials include the flour, sugar, milk, eggs, paper wrappers, and other "consumables"; the shop building, display cases, ovens and other equipment represent capital inputs; finally, advertising, insurance, and janitorial assistance represent inputs in the services category.

Personnel costs. It is difficult to think of any goods or services that an organization might produce that do not require an expenditure of time on the part of personnel. We also know that goods and services take differing amounts of time and energy to get out the door. Some industries and activities are traditionally labor intensive, such as hospitals, government agencies, textile and garment industries, and airline reservation systems. Other organizations require very little labor to produce their goods and services; examples here might be the handling of long distance phone calls, automated highway toll booths, space flights, and water treatment facilities. But, regardless of the overall level of labor expended, virtually all activities that managers or researchers will be working with have some significant labor factor. Because personnel time is often a major cost in production, it is one of the key variables in measuring productivity. In many measurement settings, it is the only input variable considered.

In earlier chapters we have discussed the importance of analyzing the larger production process into subcomponents so that intermediate outputs can be identified. This subcomponent analysis is equally important in identifying inputs. In our doughnut shop, for instance, a very obvious personnel input is the labor needed to make and cook the doughnuts. In fact, the doughnuts themselves are an input to the retail sales (the shop counter) component of the business; it is here that the doughnuts get sold to the consumer. The retail sales component has its own personnel costs in the form of counter people. A more automated cooking system might require a less educated, and therefore less costly cook. Or, if an inefficient retail floor design requires two counter personnel, then the costs of these two counter clerks should be legitimately added into the overall costs of production even though neither person is involved in actually making the doughnuts. Obviously, if the shop could sell doughnuts with only one person, then overall productivity could be enhanced. Researchers, evaluators, managers, and others aiming to implement productivity measurement efforts must be carefully attuned to identify both immediately obvious and less direct labor inputs.

In large, complex organizations, seemingly indirect personnel costs may be more directly tied to a specific product or output. The counter salespeople in the doughnut shop are such an example. If that is the case, indirect labor should be assigned to the cost of product output. When indirect labor is not clearly assignable to a specific product such as a sales force that represents a number of varied products, its cost can be evenly distributed over each product. Including the costs of indirect labor always helps the organization think through its need for multiple management layers, especially when productivity measurement includes indirect labor costs as input to goods and services output (Lehrer 1983).

Personnel costs are usually quite accessible. For hourly personnel, time sheets and payroll contain most of the information needed. For salaried personnel, yearly compensation figures (including benefits) contain most of what is needed in figuring inputs to personnel costs. Because personnel cost information is readily available, it is often the only input measure used to track productivity. As has already been stated, using only personnel costs as inputs in organizations that are not labor intensive will yield weak productivity measures. Using it in organizations which have a balance of costs due to labor, capital and energy will yield less than powerful measures.

As the United States moves toward a service economy, the cost of labor is an increasingly major factor in organizations. Because service industries are quite people intensive, measuring organizational productivity with labor inputs is critical to organizational success.

Capital costs. The measurement of this input traces the consumption of money needed to sustain a business. Nearly all organizations require some capital funding to get started, remain productive, and survive. In addition, there are some organizations that need an extensive amount of money to remain productive. Such industries might be called "capital intensive." It is this consumption of capital that is the focus of productivity measurement for this input category.

Organizations requiring large amounts of capital might be those that constantly need to replace equipment, those with extensive need for buildings and properties, or those needing large amounts of money for basic survival. Some examples may help illustrate capital kinds of organizations. A business requiring extensive equipment investments would be a phone company. Automation has diminished the need for personnel but expanded the need for expensive and sophisticated equipment. This equipment is in a constant state of new development. The need for capital to purchase this equipment is enormous. Many decisions regarding the capital investment in new equipment are based on the productivity gains to be achieved with new equipment and technology. Knowing what current productivity is and what is to be gained is the direct result of powerful productivity measurement procedures.

This country's railroads are another example of a capital intensive industry. The huge investment needed for the purchase of land for rail right-of-ways, the need for locomotives and cars, and the cost of rails and freight handling systems are immense. Little wonder this country has seen few new railroads in the past 50 years! Because the cost is so high and profit margins so questionable, few investors can be found to start such a business. Nevertheless, productivity measurement is once again the source for determining whether those rail lines in existence today can invest in new physical resources and hope to benefit from that investment with new productivity.

Tracing the contribution of capital to improved productivity is at once a simple and yet complicated process. It is simple in that data on capital expenditures is usually easy to determine. The accounting books of an organization are quite complete in this area. The complication in assessing capital's contribution to productivity is that capital investments are often useful in increasing productivity in several areas of a company. Deciding just how much of any capital investment is directly responsible for productivity improvement can be difficult. It is one thing to measure the increased productivity that is brought about by buying a new fork lift to handle a company's products. It is another to measure the increased productivity in management, manufacturing, sales, accounting, and planning when an organization purchases a new computer system. Often, the applications of such capital innovations are difficult to trace and require more sophisticated research methods.

Energy costs. Again, few, if any, companies are totally free from energy consumption and therefore energy costs. For some organizations, measuring and increasing the productivity of energy consumed can be most helpful. By energy, we mean those resources needed to drive the production process. Examples would be natural gas, electricity, water, oil, coal, and so forth.

A company we recently worked with is in the warehousing business, specifically cold and frozen storage. Their monthly costs for electricity in summer months averaged just over $300,000. They were very interested in ways to make the energy they used more productive. Simple things like doors that automatically close in refrigeration and freezer units improved productivity. Additional insulation on walls and ceilings of the cold and freezer storage units made the energy they purchased more productive. By measuring the use of energy necessary to keep a pound of frozen products, the company could target areas of needed improvements and determine if the energy savings were likely to pay off.

Another energy consuming business is transportation. Trucking and airline industries are very conscious of their energy costs, as was evident during the panics in both industries during the oil embargoes of the 1970s. Both industries are continuously measuring their energy consumption against the pounds of freight and/or passengers moved. In either case, a 10% productivity gain in energy consumption can contribute immense profits. Measuring productivity, in this case energy inputs, can tell these industries whether equipment needs replacement, engines require tuning, or better driver/pilot training in energy conservation practices is needed.

Locating documentation for measuring energy inputs is relatively easy. Usually, either the utility company or purchasing department of the organization can tell you very accurately and quickly what energy inputs have been used. In some cases, energy use can be directly tied as an input to the production of goods and services. However, in the case of an electric or natural gas bill, it may be more difficult to tie energy use to a specific machine or procedure. Individual metering can be a solution if the potential productivity gains can offset the cost of new meters and their installation.

Material costs. Many organizations consume large amounts of raw materials in the production of goods and services. By measuring the use of material inputs in production, it is possible to know when changes in productivity occur or when changes in material handling procedures result in increased productivity. "Materials" refer to a variety of things. In a bakery, it would be flour, sugar, and yeast. In a book printing company, it would be paper and ink. In a dry cleaning business, it would be cleaning fluid. In a linen service company, it would be soap, bleach and fabric softener.

If a company can squeeze a larger number of quality goods and services out of the same material inputs, then it has increased productivity. In the case of a dry cleaning service, if two additional garments can be cleaned in a new cleaning fluid compared to one currently used and the cost for both fluids is equal, productivity has increased. If a super yeast leavens

50 loaves of bread compared to 35 for the old yeast, productivity may again have increased if the cost for the two yeasts is comparable.

Material inputs can be raw materials or intermediate finished goods that are used in creating the organization's final outputs. Consider, for example, that in the making of computer circuit boards, tiny microchips are installed. In the current assembly process, 3 out of every 100 chips are ruined by the soldering action used to install them. If an inexpensive way can be found to reduce the destroyed chip count in circuit board assembly to zero or 1 in 100, productivity has taken an upturn. It is the productivity measurement system, specifically the measurement of inputs, that has shown where productivity could be increased and whether a solution produced the gains expected.

Service inputs. Service inputs represent those costs for indirect resources necessary in the production of the goods or the provision of services whose productivity is the focus for improvement. As noted earlier in the example of the doughnut shop, service inputs included advertising, liability insurance, and public relations. These are vital components of the overall doughnut shop business but are not readily identified from an analysis of the production or sales process. Nonetheless, they represent costs and also represent potential targets for measurement and cost reduction. In a large company, there may be many such service inputs, such as those provided by a personnel unit, legal department, cafeteria, recreation service, and even the myriad layers of higher management. It is important to identify these service inputs where they exist and consider their inclusion in a measurement scheme.

GUIDELINES FOR IDENTIFYING INPUT MEASURES

Input measurement can be directed to primary inputs—those resources used in any initial production process—or intermediate inputs. Intermediate inputs are those inputs consumed in latter processes and are provided as the result of preceding processes. Earlier in the book, readers will recall, we noted the example of a carwash. In the carwash, washed cars are the output of the "washing" component and are provided as material inputs to the "waxing" component. If these cars are not completely washed, have been damaged in washing, or have been re-soiled in transit to waxing, then the waxing component receives a sub-standard input, and productivity suffers. Sometimes, measurement of intermediate inputs implicates problems in prior processes (poor washing, for example); other times, it may indicate where problems in the handling or storage of the intermediate inputs (washed cars, for example) can lead to productivity improvements.

The procedures by which inputs are obtained, stored, handled, and routed to the processes that use them can yield productivity gains as well. A noteworthy example of this is the concept of "just-in-time inventory" (sometimes called "zero-stocks"). Traditionally, manufacturers maintained large stocks of materials used in production, much as a homeowner might stock a pantry with canned goods or baking ingredients. Modern "just-in-time" approaches use computers to calculate and schedule production needs and to order necessary raw materials "just-in-time" for use, thus reducing storage costs, risks of damage, costs of inventory, protection, and so forth. This concept has created very significant productivity improvements and derives directly from the concept of identifying and measuring inputs.

The selection of inputs for measurement and inclusion in productivity indices is a critical concern. Relatively speaking, it is easier to identify outputs for measurement than it is to identify inputs; there are fewer outputs, and those few outputs of most significance to customers are quite readily apparent. On the other hand, production of an output involves dozens of inputs. If, for example, we wished to increase the productivity of the doughnut shop, which inputs should we choose for measurement: baking staff? counter personnel? energy? ancillary services? materials? The answer, of course, is that we should choose those few inputs most critical to the production process, and those which provide the most leverage for productivity improvement.

In the example of the bakery, for instance, we might identify baking powder as input. Yet baking powder, because it is relatively cheap, readily available, and is used in small quantities provides very little leverage for productivity improvement. Even if we were to make a major revision to this input or perhaps even delete it altogether, we would see only a minimal gain in productivity. On the other hand, if we could reduce cooking time in half, we might save very significant amounts of energy—a major cost factor.

The point here is that managers, researchers, and evaluators have to spend considerable time and thought in selection of the critical few inputs for measurement that are likely to yield the greatest potential for productivity improvement. To this end, we provide some guidelines intended to be helpful in the identification of input measures.

Look Beyond the Use of Personnel Costs as the Input Measure

Our experience has shown that many organizations see improved productivity coming from personnel efforts only. When asked for their productivity indices, many reveal that the only input measured is labor or personnel costs. In companies we have worked with, specifically those switching to improved process technology, their greatest productivity gains have been achieved through a combination of capital, materials and personnel. Only those organizations which are labor intensive should look first to personnel costs as the critical input measure in a productivity system. Even then, it is wise to consider other aspects of input costs.

Personnel costs are often used as the input measure because they are so easy to track, are rather easy to attach to produced goods or services, and often are the easiest input to blame for poor productivity. Material, energy, and capital costs are generally under the control of senior management. It is easier to point to the bottom level of the organization than the top when productivity falls.

**Measure First Those Inputs of the Measurement Process
That Can Be Directly Tied to the
Production of the Output Goods and Services**

The most useful input measures include inputs that can be easily and clearly tied to a produced output. If the number and quality of doughnuts produced consumes personnel time, materials and energy, then all three elements could be included in the productivity measurement system. If the quantity and quality of relayed telephone calls consumes major amounts of capital and materials, then those elements should be the inputs to any productivity measurement system.

When all of the inputs are included in the productivity index, it is referred to as "total productivity measurement." When any less than all five input measures are used, it is referred to as "partial productivity measurement." For those beginning to measure productivity, we would suggest that you start with a partial productivity measurement system. In a legal department's report production process, for example, it may be very useful to measure only word processing costs because if these costs were reduced, major productivity gains would be achieved. Recall that we believe that measuring productivity, even with less than perfect accuracy, is better than no productivity measurement. Creating the perfect system, or even trying to, will probably lead to no system at all.

**Use Available Data for Input
Measures Whenever Possible**

If you have readily available data on personnel costs/time, material and energy costs, or captial expenditures, use it before creating an elaborate data gathering system. Remember—productivity measurement consumes time and resources. Minimize those costs so that gains made in productivity because of measurement and tracking are enhanced. As you become a master at productivity measurement, you will quickly see the need to capture data in any new process so that productivity measurement is made possible. Until then, try to live with what is available. This makes it easier to sell to top management and other research sponsors. Ask if you can use the data that is already available. Often the data has been collected, but no one really understands how it can be used to help build an effective and efficient company.

Keep the First Input Measurement Attempt Simple

If time and resources are not available for fully developed input measures, begin with one simple input measure, one that you are sure is responsible for output productivity, and track that input effectively. As the process proves useful, support for such efforts will be generated. With additional time and resources, more sophisticated input measurement systems can be developed. This guide suggests that a partial productivity measurement system may be most useful when starting.

Identify Inputs That Enable Maximum Leverage

As was noted earlier, some inputs have a greater bearing on the quality or quantity of outputs. Energy use in baking doughnuts is more of a major factor, for example, than baking powder. On the other hand, it makes little sense to measure even a major input if there is little control over it. A nuclear reactor, for example, requires given amounts of radioactive materials, and these are highly regulated by federal agencies as well as being cost-controlled. There is little, if anything, that management can do to make revisions in this input's cost or acquisition factors; it is largely a "given," and productivity measurement could be more usefully focused elsewhere.

MEASURING INPUTS

As with outputs, there are a variety of methods by which input consumption and characteristics can be measured. We list and briefly discuss in the following section some of the more common methods that we, and other researchers and managers, have relied upon.

1. Analysis of Documents and Records

The typical organization is replete with (if not overburdened by) documents such as forms, requisition copies, and so forth that provide a record of the consumption of resources. Utility bills, for instance, provide a record of how much money has been spent on energy costs; payroll records show how much has been spent on salaries and wages. The log sheet taped to the side of a copying machine or the sign-out sheet typically found pasted on the inside of a stationery supply closet are further examples of such readily accessible input measurement sources.

Usually, these records are readily available and are usually quite accurate as well. Researchers and others wishing to access these records to derive inputs need to design aggregation and analysis forms, but often this is the extent of the instrumentation task.

2. Direct Observation and Inspection

It is common practice in many manufacturing settings for workers to regularly (either on random or systematic bases) select a sample of some critical material resource so that it can be analyzed and measured on a number of dimensions. A bolt manufacturer may, for example, regularly pull a sample of raw steel bolt stock and subject it to tests to assess and verify its strength, flexibility, and so forth. Road construction crews take a sample of the concrete delivered to a work site and conduct a series of tests to determine the concrete's consistency and composition to assure that it meets rigid quality criteria.

In a similar approach, a publisher might review manuscripts submitted by authors to see whether they adhere to format guidelines, are free of typing errors, use acceptable graphics, and so forth. Such measures indicate whether inputs are suitable for use in the production process, and whether productivity gains might be realized by demanding more stringent quality from suppliers.

3. Analysis of Budgets and Cost-Projection Reports

Budgets and similar reports provide a less accurate documenation of actual expenditure of resources than do expenditure records. But such reports are often more accessible and less expensively obtained and should be considered. Depending on the budgeting process used in the organization, a budget document may, in fact, represent a very accurate picture of expenditures. Budget reports are particularly useful when accuracy demands are not particularly high, but the researcher or manager needs a quick and gross estimate of input allocation.

4. Self Reports, Logs, and Diaries

Personnel inputs are often tracked and accounted for by the use of logs or other similar devices. A traveling salesperson, for example, maintains a mileage and sales-call log; attorneys keep logs of how much time was spent on telephone calls or other activities for specific clients; consultants keep travel and appointment logs. These logs and diaries are a readily accessible and unobtrusive data source for a variety of personnel input functions. Where such logs are not already maintained, it is usually not a major task to have personnel keep records of when, where, what, or how they have expended their time. In sum, logs and diaries are a useful and appropriate data source.

5. Interviews and Surveys

Interviews and surveys may be designed to gather either opinions and estimates of resource expenditure, or they may be designed to ask participants to recall and reconstruct resource expenditures. In either case, these survey methods can be very useful in retrieving information where it is not otherwise available. A problem with their use is, of course, one of accuracy. Personnel may not accurately recall such data, or they may intentionally (or even unconsciously) alter their recollections and opinions for any number of reasons. A security employee who knows, for example, that it is very important to make an hourly patrol of company property, may misinterpret the amount and nature of time spent on patrol in order to avoid the possibility of punishment or censure. Nonetheless, where anonymity or some other assurances can counter the temptation to misrepresent, survey methods can be a useful device for measuring resource expenditure.

6. Automated Metering and Measuring

Many machines and electronic devices already have, or can be easily adapted to incorporate, automatic usage metering devices. The copier in our department, for example, has a metering unit that counts the number of copies made and also reports on the number and date of copies made by each authorized user. Telemarketing operations using automated call distribution systems employ a small but powerful computer that produces very sophisticated reports as to when calls were made or received, their duration, frequency, and so forth. For a simpler, lower technology example, consider the water or gas meter on a building. All such devices measure and maintain some record of resource use and are usually readily accessible.

7. Artifact Analysis, and Other Unobtrusive Measures

We once needed to estimate the extent to which trainees in a series of training sessions relied upon and made use of the many different materials provided them. For a while, we relied on a survey report from the trainees themselves. On one such survey we asked the trainees if they had used materials that we in fact hadn't handed out for three years. We found that they said that they used and relied on these handouts. We knew we had not collected reliable data. About the same time, a training staff member had to rummage through the trash bin outside the training room to search for a missing airline ticket, and discovered therein great quantities of a number of handouts we had given trainees. A regular analysis of trash bin contents gave us a good estimate of which materials were truly retained by the trainees.

Because many tangible resources and tools often show traces of their use, an analysis of wear and tear, or other evidence of use, can provide an accurate measure of resource expenditure. The frequency of repair or replacement of consumable parts, the quantity of residuals (such as, the amount of handouts left in cans), or other such traces are often a highly objective and direct measure of use, or scrap, rates.

In sum, there are a number of methods available to researchers and others who want to measure input consumption. As with any measure, making a choice should be guided primarily by what method will yield the most useful data at the cheapest cost, and with the greatest degree of accuracy.

ILLUSTRATED INPUTS

In Chapter 4, we illustrated numerous output measures for a variety of jobs. Using some outputs from that same list, we list here some input measures that could be used for those same job outputs:

	$$\frac{Output}{Input}$$
Individual Performer	
Warehouse handler	$$\frac{\text{Pounds placed in storage without damage}}{\text{Handler hours + hours of forklift use}}$$
Salesperson	$$\frac{\text{New accounts opened and retained}}{\text{Salesperson salary + travel costs}}$$
Secretary	$$\frac{\text{Number of letters typed without error}}{\text{Secretarial hours + cost of word processor/day}}$$
Shipping clerk	$$\frac{\text{Pounds shipped on time to correct address}}{\text{Freight charges + clerk's hours}}$$
Data processing manager	$$\frac{\text{Number of timely, accurate reports}}{\text{Computer costs of generating reports}}$$
Pastor	$$\frac{\text{Number of trained hospital visitors}}{\text{Pastor's salary}}$$
Professor	$$\frac{\text{No. of credit hours reported by satisfied students}}{\text{Salary costs + cost of classroom space}}$$

Machine Performer	
Grinding machine	$$\frac{\text{Number of units ground to specific tolerance daily}}{\text{Cost of machine/day + electric costs to run}}$$
Photocopy machine	$$\frac{\text{Number of quality copies/month}}{\text{Cost of photocopier/month}}$$
Blast furnace	$$\frac{\text{Number of pounds of molten ore produced}}{\text{Material costs + energy costs}}$$

Unit Performance	
Personnel department	$$\frac{\text{Number of viable applicants in pool}}{\text{Cost of ads}}$$
Accounting department	$$\frac{\text{Number of timely, accurate reports}}{\text{Accountant time + computer costs}}$$
Cereal maker	$$\frac{\text{Pounds of salable cereal product made}}{\text{Cost of grain + Labor cost + Processing cost}}$$

Organizational Performance	
Retail sporting goods	$$\frac{\text{Sales dollars (adjusted for inflation)}}{\text{Cost of production + cost of sales activities}}$$

Temporary help agency $\dfrac{\text{Number of complaint-free hours delivered}}{\text{Cost of service scheduling}}$

Health club $\dfrac{\text{Number of memberships gained or lost}}{\text{Cost of marketing efforts}}$

These are only samples of input measures tied to outputs in diverse organizations. Other input measures could be used. They could also be powerful in shaping improved productivity efforts.

SUMMARY

In this chapter, we have defined inputs in productivity measurement processes, identifying five major input categories: personnel, capital, energy, materials, and services. We have demonstrated how to choose which inputs are measured and reviewed a variety of measurement approaches.

We have also shown that productivity measurement can occur as a "partial" or "total" measure. When all inputs are included in the production of outputs, total productivity is measured. When less than all four factors are included, the system is only a partial measure. Lastly, the chapter closed with a listing of several examples of inputs.

6

A Sampler of Productivity Measure Formats

In this chapter we present and discuss a range and variety of productivity measure formats. The purpose of the chapter is to acquaint the reader with a number of productivity measure types and structures. To keep the chapter to a manageable length, we have sought here to present and discuss only a relatively few primary and prototypical measure formats. There are dozens of variations that could be constructed for each of the primary types.

The chapter begins with the most simple measurement formats, and progresses to more complex, multi-attribute formats. Considerable narrative discussion accompanies each measure, pointing out its structural highlights, similarities and differences with other measure formats, and its strengths and weaknesses as a productivity index format.

The reader should not approach this chapter as a ''catalog'' from which measures can be selected, ready-made, to be used fruitfully. None of the measures we include here can be used as they are. The most useful measures for particular settings will probably incorporate elements from one or more of the format types presented here. The construction of practical productivity measures often requires considerable creativity, and always requires customization to meet the unique demands of particular applications.

For purposes of clarity and simplicity, all of the measures in this chapter relate to a single example: a clinical testing unit within a large pharmaceutical manufacturing and sales company. The unit's mission is to collect critical trial information from physicians around the world, and compile this information into reports for use by managers within the company, as well as for several external regulatory agencies. The particular content of the reports is not relevant, and so is intentionally left unspecified. It is sufficient for the reader to assume and note that, in this continuing example, report content is meant to be accurate and timely, and is meant to be used in a variety of helpful ways (to gain licenses for distribution, or to change sales strategies, for instance) by customers of the clinical trials reporting unit.

The measures presented and discussed first are measures of output only. They are not, according to the definition presented in Chapter 2, true productivity measures. Consideration of these output-only measures provides a useful starting point, and enables us to highlight some of the critical strengths and weaknesses of the true productivity formats that follow.

OUTPUT MEASURE VARIATIONS

The measure below presents only the most simple of output information.

Number of Reports Produced Per Month

Month	Number
Sept.	60
Oct.	66
Nov.	60
Dec.	54

This measure is strictly quantitative. It provides no indication of report quality (utility, accuracy, timeliness, and so forth). As such, it presents only very limited information as to quantity of unit production. Since production volume may normally fluctuate, the measure format is not helpful in reaching any conclusions about how well the unit is doing, such as whether it is ahead of or behind schedule. There is no inclusion of an input factor, so of course this measure is nowhere near being an index of productivity.

What the measure does show, is that the unit is capable of measuring its production, which is, of course, a precondition for productivity measurement. That the measure exists at all tells us that the unit has defined what is, or is not, a "report," and that it has adopted some method for counting its production on a monthly basis.

Consider this next variation:

Unit Report Production

Month	Number	% change	% of Targeted Goal for Month
Sept.	60	–	100%
Oct.	66	+10%	90%
Nov.	60	-9%	100%

This measure, while still not a productivity index, provides considerably more information. First, it clarifies the month-to-month trend by including a percentage to reflect the change from the prior month. The significance of the trend is suggested by the indication as to the extent to which actual production has met expected production. Thus, one can note that for October, while production rose (a seemingly positive indicator), apparently the unit did not perform as well as expected, since the expectation for October was that slightly more than 73 reports should have been produced. The 66 reports represented only 90% of the expectation for that month.

While not providing any indication of the quality of the reports themselves, this measure does suggest something about the quality of the unit's performance, in that it shows the extent to which the unit met its production goals. But it is important to see how this indication of unit performance falls short of a more substantial indication of quality. The quality of each report, it we apply a "fit for use" definition, would be best estimated by applying some criteria, and these criteria should be derived from customer needs and expectations for the reports. Assume, for example, that the sales and marketing unit uses clinical test data to formulate marketing brochures for physicians. Clearly, this unit (a customer of the reporting unit) needs very accurate information that is conveyed in a clear and understandable format. Thus, a measure of the reports' quality should gauge, at a minimum, the accuracy and clarity of the reports. However, the example measure incorporates no such assessment of these critical quality dimensions. We see only that the reporting unit has met, or not met, some possibly arbitrary and even irrelevant production quota, that may or may not have anything to do with customer needs or expectations.

Again, it should be noted that this sample measure incorporates no estimate of resources (input) expended, and thus is not a productivity measure. It measures only output quantity.

Measures of unit performance such as the measure above can be very useful, despite the shortcomings discussed earlier. Certainly, it is important for unit managers to set unit goals, and to provide feedback on how well the unit meets such goals. And, if unit goals are established in ways that include valid estimates of customer needs, then reports about goal achievement are equally valid indicators of success. Likewise, if measures of production have been constructed to reflect only production that meets quality criteria (such as counting only complete and accurate reports in production totals), then measures like that shown above look increasingly better. And again, as we noted earlier, being able to define, assess, and report unit production is a crucial precondition for being able to move further, and create unit productivity measures. Clearly, a unit manager who cannot even define and assess the unit's outputs such that they can be counted in the first place is going to have a difficult time measuring unit productivity. And, chances are, a unit wherein unit output is so ill defined as to defy recognition and counting is likely to be suffering from some serious productivity problems anyway!

Output Quality Measures

A measure of output can be easily redesigned to reflect output quality, thus avoiding many of the shortcomings associated with measures of output quantity only, as they were discussed in the preceding paragraphs. Consider the measure below:

$$\frac{\text{number of reports successfully completed}}{\text{number of reports completed}}$$

This simple ratio measure incorporates a quality dimension, as it expresses the proportion of all reports written that are deemed "successful." The closer this ratio is to 1.00, then the greater the quality of the unit's performance in report writing.

The first note of importance to comment on here is that this quality measure has to be preceded by some measurement. That is, all reports completed have to be first counted, then assessed against some quality criteria to see which reports are "successful." For example, each report can be rated by the customers who receive the report, using the example checklist below:

1. Did you receive the report on time?   ( ) yes   ( ) no
2. Was the report error free?   ( ) yes   ( ) no
3. Was the report understandable?   ( ) yes   ( ) no
4. Did the report contain the information you needed? ( ) yes   ( ) no

Only a report receiving all "yes" responses would be deemed a successful report.

It should also be noted that this ratio measure, while it expresses quality, does not reflect quantity. The unit could have produced 100 reports, all of acceptable quality (thereby "successful"), and this would have earned a ratio score of 1.00.

$$\frac{\text{100 successful reports}}{\text{100 reports completed}}$$

Likewise, only one report written, if it were successful, would earn the same 1.00 score. And, this ratio measure says nothing about whether the number of reports completed during the measurement period was indicative of good, or bad, unit performance. That is, the measure does not reflect the extent to which the unit produced an acceptable number of reports, or whether production should have been less, or greater. To address this problem, however, it would be simple to add a quantity measure such as those presented earlier in this section.

Or, the ratio measure could be modified to include a goal achievement factor, such as that below:

$$\frac{\text{number of successful reports}}{\text{no. of reports completed} + (\text{unit report no. goal} - \text{no. of reports completed})}$$

If, for example, the unit goal were to produce 200 reports, but only 100 were completed, all of which were successful, then:

$$\frac{100 \text{ successful reports}}{100 \text{ reports} + (200 \text{ goal} - 100 \text{ reports})}$$

or

$$\frac{100}{100 + 100} = .50$$

In this example, the factor in the parentheses "punishes" failure to meet unit goals, by reducing the overall performance index by an arbitrary, but consistent factor. The problem with a combined measure such as this is that it masks the extent to which unit performance is affected by failure to meet quality goals or failure to meet quantity goals. Assuming that both quality and quantity are equally important, then this masking is not an issue. But, if quality is more important than quantity, then it becomes difficult to construct a measure that reflects this different value; in such instances, it would be best to rely on two separate measures—one for quality, and one for quantity and goal achievement.

The last comment to make about this ratio quality measure is that it incorporates no input factor. It is not, thus, a true productivity measure. It remains, however, a very useful index of quality.

TRUE PRODUCTIVITY RATIOS

It is not difficult to restructure the quality ratio presented in the preceding paragraphs so that it reflects productivity.

$$\frac{\text{number of reports completed successfully}}{\text{number of all reports} \times \text{average \$ cost per report}}$$

A cost factor has been added to the simple quality ratio, and so this measure now reflects productivity. If, for example, the unit produces the same number of reports each month, and keeps quality consistent, then this measure will indicate a productivity gain: less costs per successful report. Or, the unit could gain productivity by keeping costs constant, or even letting them increase some, if greater quality (more successful reports among all reports completed) were achieved. In other words, this measure is sensitive to productivity changes caused either by changes in cost, or changes in quality. (The cost factor in this measure, because it reflects dollar values, would have to be regularly adjusted for inflation or productivity estimates would be biased.)

It is useful to note that the average cost per report estimate could have been a carefully assessed and accurate figure based on thorough cost tracking, or it could have been a rough, but informed, estimate. As was discussed in Chapter 5 (Input Measurement) such rough estimates can be useful, as long as they are consistent from application to application.

As it is constructed, the ratio gives an estimate of the number of successful reports completed per unit of cost. If, for instance, the results are:

$$\frac{10 \text{ successful reports}}{20 \text{ reports completed} \times \$200 \text{ average cost per report}}$$

Or

$$\frac{10}{\$4,000} = \frac{1}{\$400}$$

That is, for example, "$100 yields .25 successful reports. The ratio could be inverted to reflect costs per successful report, or "Cost per successful report = $400."

This measure incorporated a total cost factor. Partial factors, however, are commonly used. For example:

$$\frac{\text{number of reports successfull completed}}{\text{number of reports written} \times \text{average secretarial hours per report}}$$

This productivity ratio is identical in format to the earlier measure, but it includes only secretarial time as the input factor. Where secretarial time is the major input, and also an input that represents a leverage point (that is, a prior investigation showed that secretarial time seemed to be too great and could be constructively reduced, with new equipment, for example, then this measure would be quite useful. Ratios such as this can be constructed to include any input factors of interest, or can combine input factors. Or several ratios, each using a different input factor, could be employed. Many variations are possible, and are limited only by the needs of the situation and the creativity of those constructing the measures.

Rework Factors

Consider this variation of the earlier measure:

$$\frac{\text{number of successful reports}}{\left[\begin{array}{c}\text{number of all}\\\text{reports}\end{array}\right]\times\left[\begin{array}{c}\text{average cost per}\\\text{initial report}\end{array}\right]+\left[\begin{array}{c}\text{number of reports}\\\text{reworked}\end{array}\right]\times\left[\begin{array}{c}\text{average cost of}\\\text{each rework}\end{array}\right]}$$

The input (denominator) factor in this measure has been partitioned into two major elements. The first is an initial cost element, which represents all of the costs incurred in producing the initial version of each report. The second element is a "rework" factor, which includes the costs incurred in reworking any reports that need corrections. The rework cost represents the expenses necessitated by poor quality initial work; it is the cost needed to transform a flawed report into a "successful" report.

The power of this measure is that it highlights the critical nature of quality, and clearly demonstrates the truth of the statement, "defects are not free." As the measure shows, it costs money to produce a defective report. It then costs more money to transform a defective report into a successful report.

Note that the measure reflects productivity gains and losses in several ways. Productivity may be gained by:

1. a greater proportion of successful reports overall
2. an increase in the proportion of initially acceptable reports
3. a decrease in the cost of producing initial reports
4. a decrease in the costs of reworking defective reports
5. some combination of the changes listed above (1-4)

Because the measure reflects separate productivity elements, it enables a manager to track and assess the effectiveness of different efforts to improve productivity. As is obvious, for instance, the manager might try to reduce the number of reports that need rework by improving accuracy in initial reports. Or, the manager might leave initial report success at the level it is, and try to reduce the costs of producing initial reports. It might even be the case, however, that an overall productivity gain could be achieved by tolerating a greater number of initially defective reports. The costs of producing a more hasty and incorrect first version could be more productive, if rework costs are significantly lower than initial production costs. Whatever the effective combination of changes, be they rework costs or initial report accuracy, it is the format of this productivity index that enables identification and assessment of the several factors.

While the rework factor measure provides more specific information than the single input factor measure, it is important to reflect briefly on its shortcomings. Again, we remind the reader that any productivity measure necessarily reduces highly complex phenomena to simple, basic, narrow concreteness. Consider, for example, that the reporting unit manager decides, based on measurement information, that it is possible to improve overall productivity by tolerating a higher number of initial reports needing rework. That is, the manager determines that it is cheaper to fix up initial reports than it is to make them perfect on the first try. So far, so good; the measure indicates the economic sense of the manager's argument. Nonetheless, it still might be a bad idea to adopt this strategy, even though it will apparently result in productivity improvement. There may be a host of other "costs" associated with this strategy not reflected by the measure. Initial report writers may find it demoralizing to work more sloppily, and thus their productivity in other tasks may suffer. Or, there may be a risk that a flawed report could be mistakenly disseminated, because quality assessment procedures are not perfect. If this risk is great, and could produce dire consequences, then the apparent productivity gain may not be worth it.

The bottom line here for all productivity measure formats is that the measures provide useful, but not complete, information. Productivity measurement data are tremendously useful. But, they cannot and should not replace management judgment. The unit manager must be fully aware of the political, social, psychological, and economic context, in order to make truly sound productivity improvement decisions.

Multi-Factor Measures

The measures that follow are considerably more complex than the preceding examples. The multi-factor measures are also called "matrix" measures because of their two dimensional format. As will be seen, these measures partition the output (numerator) element into several levels, and incorporate scoring systems to rate output quality on a numerical scale.

Figure 6.1 displays the timeliness of each report along the horizontal dimension, and uses the vertical dimension to show separate timeliness scores

Kind of Report	Average Time For Report Successfully Completed											SUMMARY CHART		
	TIME SPECIFICATIONS											Score	Weight	Rating
	Over					Right On	Under							
	More Than 20%	15-20%	11-15%	6-10%	1-5%	On	1-5%	6-10%	11-15%	16-20%	More Than 20%			
1) Major Audits	0	1	2	3	4	5	6	7	8	9	10		4	
2) Inspections	0	1	2	3	4	5	6	7	8	9	10		3	
3) Informed Consent	0	1	2	3	4	5	6	7	8	9	10		2	
4) Single Regulation Checks	0	1	2	3	4	5	6	7	8	9	10		1	

TOTAL INDEX = ⁼⁼⁼⁼⁼

Figure 6.1. Monthly Report Time Average

for each of four types of reports the unit produces: major audits, inspections, informed consent reports, and simple regulation check reports.

Each type of report has been assigned a "weight" factor. As can be seen in the measure, "major audits" have been assigned a weight factor of 4; "inspections," deemed less important by the unit, have a weight factor of 3, and so on. The notion at work here is that some outputs (in this case, kinds of reports), have differing degrees of importance to the unit producing them. The degree of importance could be established from a customer perspective, from the difficulty in producing the report, from the quantity of resources the report consumes, or some combination of these or other factors. The measure also incorporates a "score" based on how timely the report is—whether it is produced later than, or earlier than, the timeliness criteria established by the unit. Note that this score is an average, calculated monthly, for each type of report. As Figure 6.2 indicates (by the circled number on the 0-10 point scale for each report type), "major audits" during the month shown were completed an average of 11-15% earlier than the time specifications for major audits, and thus earned a timeliness score of "8" for the month. "Inspection" reports, on the other hand, were an average of 1-5% late, earning a "4"; the remaining two report types eaerned scores of "5," since they were neither earlier nor later than the criteria established for them. Report scores were then tallied under the "score" column in the box at the right hand edge of the measure format. These earned scores were then multiplied by the "weight" factor to yield a monthly rating for each report type. These ratings were then totalled, to yield a single unit report timeliness index for the month. The single report timeliness index could be charted each month, as shown in Figure 6.3. As the chart shows, the unit has generally increased the timeliness of reports for each month, with the exception of a decrease in July; then, following July is a major increase in timeliness, with a slight decrease and flattening of the trend line. This chart shows how a single index such as this is useful for reflecting general production trends. The matrix measure format calculated each month is useful for showing, in greater detail, how each type of report contributed to or detracted from, that month's performance.

There are several items of interest to note in this sort of measure format:

1. The measure is not a productivity measure, since it incorporates no input factor. Further, the quality factor is somewhat limited, relating only to timeliness.
2. Weight factors are relative, and represent a subjective judgment. They can be determined from any number of perspectives, such as importance to

Kind of Report — Average Time Over/Under Unit Specifications for Reports

Kind of Report	Over More Than 20%	Over 15-20%	Over 11-15%	Over 6-10%	Over 1-5%	Right On	Under 1-5%	Under 6-10%	Under 11-15%	Under 16-20%	Under More Than 20%
1) Major Audits	0	1	2	3	4	5	6	7	(8)	9	10
2) Inspections	0	1	2	3	(4)	5	6	7	8	9	10
3) Informed Consent	0	1	2	3	4	(5)	6	7	8	9	10
4) Single Regulation Checks	0	1	2	3	4	(5)	6	7	8	9	10

	Score	Weight	Rating
	8	4	3 2
	4	3	1 2
	5	2	1 0
	5	1	5

TOTAL INDEX   59

Figure 6.2. Monthly Report Time Average

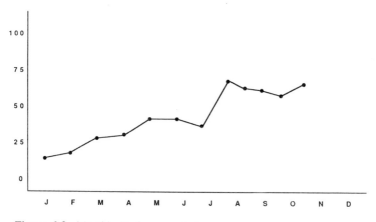

Figure 6.3. Monthly Performance Index

customers, profitability of the output, difficulty of production, political visibility, degree of risk, and so forth.

3. The format produces a single numerical index, but also displays more detailed information about how each output contributed to the index.

4. Considerable measurement and planning has preceded an index of this sort. Weights, for example, must be established. And, a procedure for measuring the timeliness of each report against some criterion must be established. Most commonly, this weighting is determined by spending time with the units' customers. They can best determine the quality criterion.

5. Because the final index is calculated using value weights from which raw scores are multiplied, any given index score could have been earned in more than one way. Minor decreases in timeliness of highly weighted reports could be offset by major timeliness changes in less important report types. Or, the opposite may be true. For this reason, matrix score indices can be hard to interpret. Thus, keeping records on the matrix, which documents the construction of the index, is important.

6. The dimension along the horizontal axis (report timeliness) could be any other measured qualitative dimension, such as accuracy, relevance of content, readability, and so forth.

As was noted, a matrix measure such as this is not a true productivity measure, because no input factor is incorporated. The measure could be used in conjunction with other productivity measures to provide a more complete picture of unit operation and effectiveness. Or, the index score could be used as the numerator in a new index whose denominator is a total, partial, or a rework estimate of input.

Figure 6.4 is another example of a matrix measure. Here, a more complete estimate of output quality is reflected, since only those reports deemed "successful" are included. In other words, this measure does not track the timeliness of reports that are not up to previously established unit quality criteria.

The amount and nature of measurement that would have to precede this measure format is considerable. Notice that this measure displays timeliness (as did the previous example), and so incorporates some procedure for measuring report timeliness prior to recording these results on the matrix. Likewise, there has been some prior assessment of the quality of each report, since only "successful" reports have earned inclusion on the matrix.

Again, this example measure is not a true productivity measure, since there is no input factor. But this is a very useful means of recording and reflecting output quality and timeliness. As such, the matrix measure produces a highly informative and detailed "numerator." That is, the index can be used in a ratio, as below:

$$\frac{\text{index}}{\text{input costs}}$$

This ratio now provides a true productivity measure. And, when accompanied by the matrix format, it gives useful information about the changes in timeliness for various report types that contributed to changes in overall productivity. The matrix measure, when used as part of a family of similar measures, is a very useful and informative format.

SUMMARY

Productivity measures are "summary" measures, in that they are built upon preceding measures of inputs and outputs. Even a simple productivity ratio, such as:

$$\frac{\text{number of successful reports}}{\text{amount of secretarial labor}}$$

subsumes a considerable measurement effort. To create this ratio, it was necessary to define successful, versus unsuccessful, reports and establish some accurate means of assessing reports to determine whether they are successful, or not successful. Further, the productivity ratio above includes a prior measure of effort, distinguishing "secretarial" labor from all other inputs.

SUMMARY CHART

Kind of Report	# Successful	Score	Weight	Rating
1) Major Audits	3	8	4	9 6
2) Inspections	4	4	3	4 8
3) Informed Consent	2	5	2	2 0
4) Single Regulation Checks	3	5	1	1 5

TOTAL INDEX 179

Average Time Over/Under Unit Specifications for Reports

Kind of Report	Over More Than 20%	15-20%	11-15%	6-10%	1-5%	Right On	1-5%	6-10%	11-15%	16-20%	Under More Than 20%
1) Major Audits	0	1	2	3	4	5	6	7	(8)	9	1 0
2) Inspections	0	1	2	3	(4)	5	6	7	8	9	1 0
3) Informed Consent	0	1	2	3	4	(5)	6	7	8	9	1 0
4) Single Regulation Checks	0	1	2	3	4	(5)	6	7	8	9	1 0

Figure 6.4. Monthly Report Time Average

99

Many of the measures that precede a true productivity ratio can be useful in and of themselves. This chapter opened with a discussion of several examples of measures of output quantity, showing how these measures could be readily improved to reflect quality, as well as quantity. Such output-only measures can be useful for tracking production improvement, and also help keep a focus on improvement of quality. And, creation of such measures is a precondition to being able to construct true productivity ratios.

There are a number of productivity ratio formats available. At the simplest level, ratios such as the example in the preceding paragraph can be used to reflect quality of output as a function of partial, or total, resources expended. Variations of these simple formats were presented in the chapter that can be used to reflect rework (correction of initially defective outputs). Measures incorporating rework factors are especially useful in that they allow tracking of productivity changes from a variety of factors. Rework measures can be used alone, or in conjunction with other productivity ratios and output-only measures.

The chapter closed with a presentation of "matrix" measures that reflect multiple output types or levels. Matrix measures are considerably more complex than simple output-input ratios, but likewise provide considerably more information. The matrix measures differ also in that they typically incorporate a numerical scale which transforms unit performance into standard scores. The primary utility of matrix measures is that they provide an overall unit productivity "score." The matrix format also provides a breakdown of the calculation of the overall index, so that changes in the quantity and quality of different outputs can be tracked, and their impact on the overall score can be assessed.

All of the productivity measure formats discussed in the chapter are intended to be used in conjunction with other organization performance data; none of these measures, alone, is sufficient to enable truly informed judgments about unit productivity. Our recommendation is to use several measures in combination with others, varying formats as well as types of outputs measured.

7

Seven Steps to Unit Productivity Measures

This chapter presents and discusses seven steps for constructing measures at the unit level. Each step in the process has a discrete and tangible product that can be assessed by the unit staff, measurement consultant, or researcher to assure that it is accurate and helpful in moving the unit toward the construction of effective measures. The stepwise procedures break the measurement design process down into relatively simple and less formidable tasks to encourage progress and participation.

The presentation of the steps begins with a list of all seven steps and a brief definition of the product associated with each. Then, each step is described and discussed in more detail, including examples, with guidelines for determining whether the step has been sufficiently completed to permit beginning the next step in the procedure.

It should be noted that the partitioning of the overall measurement design process into the seven steps presented here is somewhat arbitrary. The authors have reviewed dozens of other similar processes that contain numbers of steps varying widely from a mere two or three to twenty or more discrete steps. And, in our work we have sometimes used a six-, seven-, eight-, and nine-step process. The number of steps itself is immaterial. Sometimes measurement designers, working by themselves, can create good measures immediately, without working through anything resembling a stepwise process.

Our experience in working with groups (the group process, as was noted in Chapter 3 and will be discussed again in Chapter 8, is a must) has demonstrated the invaluable utility of working with a stepwise process. The use of steps greatly simplifies the larger task, guides the work in an effective method, much as a recipe directs the cooking process, and permits assessment of progress toward the eventual goal of creating good measures. Finally, a group from an organization that completes only the first few steps, or even only the first step alone, has engaged in a process of great value that, even in the absence of creating or using measures, will very likely enhance productivity!

OVERVIEW OF THE SEVEN STEPS

Here we briefly name and define each of the seven steps. The discrete product for the step, along with general criteria for assessing the adequacy of that step's product, is included.

Step 1: Mission statement. Write a mission statement for the unit that identifies the major goals and customers of the unit. The mission statement must be complete, and be compatible with the mission of the larger organization.

Step 2: Expectations. Identify for each customer the unit's products and/or services. Expectations must clearly identify and explain quality needs and expectations held by each major customer group for the unit's products and services.

Step 3: Key outputs. Identify outputs that are important to the unit's mission, responsive to customer needs and expectations, and account for the majority of the expenditures of the unit's resources.

Step 4: Major functions. Identify and describe the major functions of the unit. These must clearly represent unit operations and inputs and explain how key outputs are produced.

Step 5: Output measurement selection. Construct measurement techniques for one or more key outputs that will produce the most practical and useful quality and productivity information.

Step 6: Input measurement selection. Construct measurement techniques for one or more key inputs that are critical to the production of the outputs selected in Step 5.

Step 7: Index construction. Construct one or more productivity measures to incorporate the output and input measures into a sensitive, practical, and useful index.

The following portions of the chapter describe each step and its criteria in more detail, and present guidelines and examples to assist with completion of the steps.

STEP 1: MISSION STATEMENT

This first step identifies and explicates the goals, customers, and market arena for the unit. As such, it clarifies the very reason-for-being of the unit, explaining whom the unit serves, and what the unit is accountable for achieving.

Here are some representative mission statements for a variety of typical organization units:

> The Sales Unit sells company products to worldwide customers in sufficient numbers and product mixes to meet customer needs and achieve suitable profits.

> The Management Information Unit helps managers throughout the company create and maintain efficient unit operations by providing practical and state-of-the art information systems and services.

> The Research Division identifies and tests effective cleaning products that will safely meet the needs of customers in the northeast area and can be marketed profitably by the company.

> The Corporate Training Unit assists company managers in the development of effective personnel.

> The Educational Leadership Department helps improve the quality of education by providing development opportunities, research, and service to educational leaders throughout the state and worldwide.

> The Manufacturing Division produces selected fire fighting devices of the highest possible quality in a safe and efficient manner in quantities sufficient to meet demands of fire fighting organizations worldwide.

Perhaps the first characteristic of these sample mission statements to be noted is their brevity. Each is only a single sentence. Brevity is important, as the intent of the mission statement is to capture the essential purpose of the unit in such a way as to reduce ambiguity, and to help unit management and staff maintain their focus on important unit goals.

Another critical feature of a mission statement is that it expresses a purpose in terms of results rather than activities. It is a well known phenomenon (for a number of complex organizational and psychological reasons) that people at work tend to increasingly lose sight of purposes and become ever more involved in activities—the steps and procedures of their work. A telephone sales clerk in a mail-order business is hired in order to serve customers and increase sales, for example. The job requires that a number of activities be completed, such as answering the telephone, completing a sales order form, maintaining a list of back-order items, and so forth. The sales clerk becomes naturally focused on doing the tasks correctly, and begins to form the notion that doing the job "right" means doing each task according to the criteria for each task. As doing the tasks correctly looms ever larger in importance, the reason the job is to be done in the first place (meeting a customer's needs and making sales) diminishes in attention and salience. This phenomenon is, of course, death for productivity, since the emphasis will be on expenditure of resources in task completion versus achieving quality results with minimal task expenditure. Mission statements should thus emphasize results, not activities, to try to counteract these anti-productive bureaucratic and psychological forces.

A second important reason for mission statements to emphasize results, and de-emphasize activities, is to provide for innovation. A mission statement that declares how a job is to be done precludes doing a job differently, thus stifling creativity and invention that could lead to dramatic productivity increases. Thus, the example mission statement for the training unit expressed the unit goal of assisting managers instead of stating that the unit provides workshops, seminars, and classes. Likewise, the mission statement for the manufacturing unit specified what the unit was responsible for producing (a quality product), instead of stating that the unit operated and maintained a variety of production equipment and machinery. The mission should not "lock in" the unit to a traditional set of activities and procedures.

A mission statement should clearly identify the market and customers a unit serves. Notice that the examples given include phrases such as "company managers," "fire fighting organizations worldwide," "educational leaders within the state and worldwide." In each instance, the market is identified by the kind of customer and by a geographic region or other indication of location. Identification of customers and market regions serves further to clearly explicate the reason for the unit's existence and clarify its intended results.

Lastly, while mission statements should focus on major results, it is important to not confuse such major results with shorter term, or process-specific, objectives. Consider, for example, the following statement: "The mission of the sales unit is to increase sales in the domestic market by 15%." This statement may represent an annual, or even longer-term objective, but is too specific, short range, and limiting to serve as a statement of mission. The mission statement must encompass the entire purpose for the existence of the unit, clearly indicating its strategic function. As such, the mission becomes a referent against which all operational decisions and objectives (such as increasing sales) can be tested; decisions and objectives must always be consistent with and supportive of the mission. When no clear knowledge of mission is shared among unit or organization personnel, then the likelihood of dysfunction—operating inconsistently with the mission—is increased, and productivity is threatened.

The mission statement of a unit must, finally, be consistent with the mission of the larger organization. Thus, after a unit mission statement is written, clarified, and agreed upon at the unit level, it should be reviewed and approved by higher level management in the organization to assess its consistency and agreement with the overall organization's mission.

STEP 2: EXPECTATIONS

As beauty is in the eye of the beholder, so quality is in the eye of the customer. Earlier in this book we noted that a very practical definition of quality is "fit for customer use." That is, quality specifications must derive from and be responsive to the needs of a customer for the quality and performance of certain products and services. If the customers of a rope company, for example, need a rope that will remain flexible in extreme cold, not rot in a wet environment, and hold at least a 500 pound load, then the rope manufacturer's quality criteria must specify certain levels of performance for flexibility, durability, and strength. If the rope company is ignorant of customer needs, it may likely produce an inferior product that will not satisfy the customer and thus not sell, or it may over-engineer its rope to specifications well beyond customer needs, thus overpricing its product and giving up sales to the competition.

Knowing customers, understanding their needs, hopes, values, and expectations, is essential to producing products and services that will satisfy customers. Such understanding, of course, cannot be guessed at, but demands frequent, informative contact with customers. Thus, this second step toward producing effective productivity measures often entails surveys, interviews, or other methods of identifying and clarifying customer expectations.

Customer needs and expectations rarely remain constant. As new products and services enter markets, and as customer lifestyles, situations, and preferences change, so do expectations for quality. The buyers of automobiles in the 1940s, before the advent of hydraulic braking systems, held considerably different expectations than today's customers who have probably never driven an auto with mechanical brakes. Even now, as computer assisted braking systems that prevent wheels from "locking up" are being refined and made increasingly available, customer expectations are again changing. The quality specifications for automobile brakes in the year 2000 will be, we can guess, quite different from those of the year 1990. Just what those quality criteria will be must be identified by any automobile manufacturer who hopes to remain productive, and thus competitive. And so, it is clear that staying in touch with customer expectations and needs must be ongoing.

The need for continuing information about customer needs is particularly critical in service businesses, where the product is customer satisfaction rather than a tangible good. As has been noted earlier in this book, and will be seen in the following chapter that provides example measures, productivity measures for service operations are not just based on customer expectations, but often incorporate direct measures of customer satisfaction into the productivity index itself.

Customer expectations and needs should be identified specifically and in as much detail as possible. Lack of detail and specific understanding will hamper efforts to create measurable and accurate quality criteria. Further, it is important that the context of the customer is identified and understood. It would be important to know, for example, that certain customers for computer services work in a medical environment, and that the computer records they use are often employed in legal hearings stemming from malpractice disputes. Thus, these customers' needs for accuracy are great, and may sometimes transcend other criteria, such as timeliness. It is only with a good understanding of the customer's context that accurate, responsive criteria can be created that will help lead to the greatest levels of customer satisfaction.

STEP 3: KEY OUTPUTS

There are many outputs produced by a typical unit within a large organization. A training unit, for example, might provide consultation services, needs analyses, seminars and workshops, training attendance reports, training attendance certificates, referrals to outside consultants, review services for training documents created in other departments, schedules for training programs, and reimbursement claims for executive travel, to name a few. Of these many outputs, only a few, or perhaps only one, might warrant measurement for use in a productivity index. Many outputs might not even warrant measurement. Consider the example of the production of training certificates. These are tangible, easily measured products. And, no doubt, measurement of their quality and production might lead to some productivity gains. But, if the production of training certificates accounts for only a small fraction (say, less than .02%) of the training unit's resource expenditure, and if training certificates are considered insignificant and unimportant to customers, then it would probably make very little sense to waste time in trying to build productivity measures for the certificates. On the other hand, increasing the supervisory skills of managers through workshops might be seen as an extremely valuable output of the unit, and might also consume a major portion of the unit's resources.

Some of a unit's outputs will be far more important than others. Importance, we should note, is a relative issue, and can be estimated only in light of mission, and customer needs (thus underlining the crucial nature of the preceding two steps). Given that resources for measuring outputs are limited, and considering the fact that resources spent on measuring productivity do not, in themselves, enhance productivity, it makes sense to strategically allocate measurement efforts and resources to only those few outputs that could really make a difference. A common rule of thumb productivity consultants follow is the "80-20 Rule": Look for that 20% of the outputs that account for at least 80% of the success of the unit.

The first step in selecting key outputs is to identify and list all of the outputs of the unit. This should be done in a "brainstorming" fashion, listing each and every output regardless of its apparent importance to mission or resource expenditure level. Then, this comprehensive list can be winnowed to only a few, by considering (1) the importance of each to the unit mission, (2) the importance of each to meeting customer needs and expectations, and (3) the relative amount of resources required to produce each output. Clearly, little productivity leverage is gained by improving efficiency or quality in outputs that cost little to produce, are insignificant to customers, or are not important to the mission of the unit.

As was noted, accurately identifying "key" outputs requires an understanding of mission and customer needs and expectations. The steps just described begin that process. To some extent, identifying key outputs is dependent on the next step in the process (analyzing unit functions). Since a key output is, by definition, "expensive" (it consumes a major share of unit resources), then a knowledge of how outputs are produced in the unit is necessary. Thus, it should be noted that these seven steps are not linear nor independent. The best creation of productivity measures is iterative, and will loop back through the seven steps several times, validating assumptions and refining and expanding definitions.

We suggest the use of three methods for identifying key outputs, and we suggest further that all three be used. These are (1) unit staff group process to identify outputs perceived as most important, most expensive, and so forth; (2) customer opinions as to which outputs of the unit are most important; and (3) analysis of unit records and budgets to determine which outputs consume the most resources.

STEP 4: MAJOR FUNCTIONS

Function analysis involves determining how the unit processes inputs to produce key outputs. The step is best explained by considering first why we bother with the step at all, since analysis of functions could involve tremendous amounts of detail and time. We want to limit function analysis to get from it only what is needed to proceed with constructing good productivity measures. Even a relatively small unit is literally chock full of activities and operations, each of which could be analyzed into excruciating detail. Productivity measurers want to be careful to avoid spending too much time in this step.

Key Inputs

One major reason that a function analysis is conducted is to identify key inputs. Key inputs are those particular resources that are used in the production of key outputs, and that have a major impact on productivity for key outputs. Several criteria distinguish "key" inputs from their mundane brethren (all other inputs). In more technical language, a key input accounts for a large share of variance in the quality or efficiency of production of a key output. Consider, for instance, our earlier example of training workshops for managers. This workshop uses, among other inputs, both pencils (used by the trainees to take notes), and a skilled management trainer, to design and deliver training sessions. Clearly, the trainer accounts for more impact on the trainees's acquisition of supervisory skills (a key output) than do the pencils. That is, using higher quality pencils is likely to yield smaller gains in output quality than is the use of higher quality trainers.

The "keyness" of an input may sometimes, but not always, be related to its relative magnitude among other inputs. That is, it is often true that an input which is relatively low in cost and number when compared against all other inputs required for a process, is also relatively less significant in its impact on quality. Consider, for example, that we wish to measure and improve the productivity of the reports produced by a secretarial unit. Secretarial labor is the largest input, and is considerably greater in magnitude and expense than, say, typewriter ribbons. And, the nature and cost of typewriter ribbons, if changed, would probably have relatively little impact on report quality than would changes in secretarial skills or efficiency. But care must be taken to not overlook seemingly minor inputs and their role in the production of key outputs. If, for example, dock builders used higher quality nails (a relatively minor input), it is possible that the docks they build would resist warping and separation for twice as long—a major quality (and thereby productivity) improvement!

Another criterion for a key input is that it be an input which can be controlled. If it is impossible, or nearly impossible, to do anything about the costs, quality, timeliness, and so forth, of an otherwise important input, then it may not be useful to select it for measurement. A telemarketing company that uses computers as an integral part of the sales process might know, for instance, that disruptions in electrical service (an important input) play havoc with procedures and result in lost sales. If, however, there is no choice, among electricity vendors, and purchase of an independent power source generator is cost prohibitive, then incorporating electricity quality and continuity into a productivity index may be fruitless. There is little advantage to be gained from measuring "givens."

Throughputs

A second major reason for conducting an analysis of the functions by which key outputs are produced is to identify potentially key "throughputs." A throughput is an interim output—something produced en route to a key output. A classic example of a throughput can be identified by considering the example of a restaurant, where an obviously key output is customer satisfaction with the meal and service. An analysis of the process by which a customer receives a meal could be portrayed as follows:

COOK PREPARES MEAL → WAITER SERVES THE MEAL →
CUSTOMER WITH MEAL

The output of the first functional component (a prepared meal) is a "throughput," as it requires further processing prior to becoming the output (a customer with a meal). That is, the prepared meal is not the final unit output; it must be served by the waiter before it becomes a customer with a meal. In this example, it may be wise to measure the throughput (the prepared meal), since potential changes in this important throughput could have a significant effect on the productivity of the larger component. Measurement of the output of the second component might lead only to improvements in the second component, thereby failing to improve productivity. That is, a friendlier waiter providing quicker service of a cold, greasy, tasteless meal is bound to have very little positive impact on customer satisfaction! As can be seen, sometimes an analysis of functions can help identify important outputs other than those that are identified by analyzing only the products and services that "exit" a unit directly into the hands of customers. There may be important productivity leverage gained from measuring, then improving, the quality of significant throughputs. And significant throughputs, of course, can be identified only from a careful analysis of the operations by which key outputs are produced.

Function analysis should identify the major activity components that are involved in the production of key outputs, as they were identified in the preceding (mission, customer expectations, and key outputs) steps. Then, each major activity component may require further analysis and sub-division until all major throughputs and inputs are clarified. This is accomplished through the familiar techniques of systems analysis, breaking larger activities into sub-activities, then identifying the particular inputs, processes, and outputs of each activity and sub-activity. See Figure 7.1 for an example of a complete input-process-output analysis of a common unit operation.

STEP 5: OUTPUT MEASUREMENT SELECTION

Once key inputs and outputs are identified, it remains to choose those few key outputs among all the outputs (now augmented by any identified throughputs) that are worth measuring. As will be explained further in Chapter 8, the authors recommend, in most cases, a strategy of "starting small." Thus, we suggest that not all the key outputs be selected for measurement. The construction of useful measures, and then actually carrying out the measurement and using the measurement data, costs time, money, and sometimes considerable anguish and effort. Thus it may be wise, particularly where systematic productivity measurement is new, to begin the process with only one, or a few, measures.

We have already covered (in Chapter 4) how output measures are constructed, and so we will not repeat that information here. It is important to re-emphasize, however, that it is almost always advisable to include dimensions of quality in the output measures. Again, quality is so intricately woven into concepts of productivity, that measures of output quantity alone, or measures that do not include important quality criteria, are very likely to be useless, or even counter-productive, for productivity improvement.

Selection of outputs for measurement should be guided by a number of criteria. While differing contexts may call for differing levels of attention to the following criteria, all should be considered at least to some extent.

1. Choose for measurement the output, or outputs, most important to the accomplishment of the unit's mission.

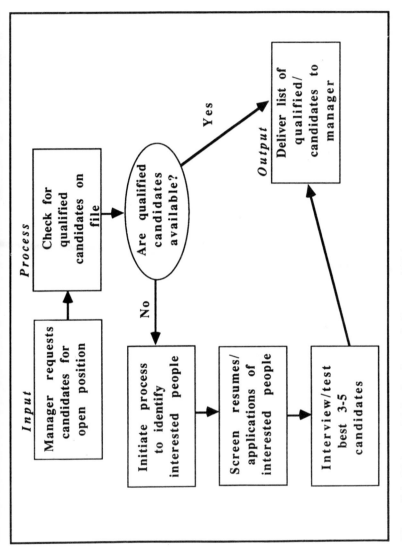

Figure 7.1. Hiring and Selection Proces in Personnel Unit

111

2. Measure the outputs for which the most measurement data are available.

3. Measure outputs for which measurement procedures would be most easy to design, conduct, analyze, and report.

4. Measure outputs that will provide the quickest "turnaround." That is, given a choice between measuring an output whose quality attributes (such a durability) will not be prominent for six months, versus an output whose quality attributes (such as timeliness) can be assessed this week, choose the output for which data can be gathered most quickly.

5. In a similar sense, choose to measure an output that recurs on a relatively frequent schedule. If changes in an output could not be begun for a relatively long period (a biannual report, for instance), it may be wiser to choose an output in which improvements could be made every month.

6. Be guided by probability for success. Do not choose to measure an output that is likely to turn up very negative, discouraging data. Likewise, do not choose for measurement an output that is highly controversial, likely to stimulate dissension and discord, and so forth. Nothing breeds success like success. Save the harder, more threatening work for later, after unit staff have had a chance to deal positively with measurement data. (See Chapter 8 for an expansion on this theme.)

7. Given a choice between measuring an output for which a useful measure would have to be relatively complex, and one which would allow a simpler measure, opt for simplicity.

8. Measure an output for which key *inputs* are known, controllable, and relatively easy to measure. This criterion looks ahead to the next step (developing measures for key inputs), and to the step after that (developing a productivity index). It is possible that a good measure of output alone, especially when it measures crucial quality dimensions, will be in itself very useful for improving productivity. In this case, one could ignore the notion of choosing an output for which inputs could be measured, since that step would not be pursued anyway. But typically, one is developing output measures for use in a productivity index, in which case at least an approximation of input expenditure is required.

In reflection, it should be evident that the choice of an output for measurement is a critical choice. It involves both technical considerations such as availability of data, ease of measurement, and relationship to variance in mission achievement; and it involves political/social criteria, such as degree of threat, likelihood of usage, and so forth. It should also be evident that the choice of a key output for measurement will involve some trade-offs. An output most central to a mission may be highly controversial, politically volatile, and hard to measure, indicating the need to choose an easier measure, more politically viable output, but one perhaps slightly less crucial to the mission.

STEP 6: INPUT MEASUREMENT SELECTION

This step is very similar in scope and process to the preceding step of choosing a key output and developing one or more measures for it. That is, among the several key inputs identified, it is now time to choose one or more for measurement. There is a crucial difference between this step and the preceding one, however: In most cases, only those inputs involved in the production of *key outputs selected for measurement* will in turn be measured. That is, it is usually not fruitful, for productivity measurement purposes, to measure and track resource expenditure in the absence of output measurement. In other words, we advise developing measures of inputs only where the measure will be used along with an output measure as part of a productivity index.

This note made, the choice of inputs for measurement should be guided primarily by the potential for payoff in a productivity index. That is, the major criterion is that the input measured be especially important to productivity; it should account for a major portion of the variance in the quality of the output (of course, if it were selected in the first place as a key input, it should already meet this criterion).

Your choice of key inputs for measurement should be further guided by the remainder of the criteria described in the preceding step (Step 5). That is, look for inputs that (1) already have available data, (2) are easily measured, (3) can be readily changed in a short time, (4) are likely to be successfully measured and used, and (5) lend themselves to simple measures.

Identification of key inputs is greatly assisted by analysis of unit budget and other records. As well, unit staff groups can be convened and their opinions as to key inputs can be gathered.

STEP 7: INDEX CONSTRUCTION

This final step involves creating productivity indices (ratios), as explained in Chapter 6, that incorporate the measurement of key outputs and inputs. The previous chapter presented and discussed a variety of productivity index formats, examples, and guidelines. Readers should refer again to that chapter for guidance in this step.

Construction of the productivity index, or indices, should be guided above all by the potential for utility. It serves little good to construct measures that cannot be used to make worthwhile decisions. The index constructed should reflect important measures of the outputs and inputs that are critically related to unit productivity.

It is often useful to develop more than one index, or a group of indices. For example, an index could be constructed for each major input used to produce one key output. For instance, in the case where the key output measured is *report quality*, one index might employ a (input) measure of "secretarial hours" as denominator, another index employ "data collection hours" as denominator, and yet another index employ "expert's review time" as the denominator. These three separate indices are likely to be more helpful in assessing and tracking productivity variation than a single index using a composite denominator that sums the three separate input factors. Similarly, it may be useful to construct several indices that each employ a different measure of output quality rather than a measure that sums (and therefore may mask) several quality dimensions.

As has been noted in preceding steps and in the preceding chapter, the index should be as simple as possible to produce, interpret, and use.

USING THE SEVEN-STEP PROCESS

As has been noted, and has been implied by cross referencing among the steps, this seven-step process is not linear. At several points it is necessary to "work ahead" on latter steps, to facilitate and validate work on prior steps. For example, the construction of key input measures is done only for those outputs for which measures are constructed, but one criterion for deciding which outputs to measure is whether it is possible to measure any important inputs for that output. Probably the only step that truly must be done first is the identification of mission and customers, for this information serves as the referent for deciding what is important, or not important.

It has also been briefly suggested that measurement work be kept simple, and that an eye toward utility be maintained. This theme has been noted in several chapters, and will be expanded in the next chapter. Some of these steps have mentioned the critical role of group process, such as in brainstorming outputs, or determining the relative importance of outputs. This reliance on group process will likewise be expanded on in the next chapter.

SUMMARY

The seven steps are intended to form a conceptual rather than a strictly procedural, guide for constructing productivity measures. It is clear that the results of each of the seven steps (the identification of key outputs, understanding of a mission, and so forth) must be achieved, clarified, and explicated. The order in which these are achieved is variable, and the overall process should be iterative. Just how one proceeds through the steps, and even whether one goes through anything distinguishable as steps, will vary from instance to instance. But in any case, the seven steps should always serve as a useful conceptual guide. The construction of good measures relies critically on the information considered and gleaned from each of the steps. Let us now turn to the final chapter, where process considerations are the central topic.

8

Productivity Measurement and the Organization: Guidelines for Success

In this final chapter, we present a number of guidelines for researchers, evaluators, and others who are seeking to implement productivity measurement efforts. These guidelines are intended primarily for those whose long range goal is to have the organization adopt and institutionalize productivity measurement systems as a "way of doing business." We recognize, however, that many readers may be seeking far less ambitious goals, such as hoping to get a client within an organization to simply try out a productivity measure or using a productivity measure as a one-time part of a larger evaluation project. But even where goals are simpler and less lofty, the guidelines we present here will be helpful, and if not followed, could often spell disaster in even the most simple of measurement efforts.

Our advice, learned from our successes as well as our fair share of failures, is that the researcher or manager always acts in congruence with these guidelines, as if the productivity measurement task were headed in the direction of eventual institutionalization even when it's a one-shot endeavor. This advice is valid primarily because the guidelines that follow stem from the larger world of evaluation and organizational intervention in general. In short, the guidelines are simply rules for good business. Further, these guidelines represent our professional bias that all evaluation and measurement efforts, regardless of current scope and objectives, should be pursued from the perspective that the ultimate goal of all applied research is to learn more about research practice and to extend research usage and applications.

GUIDELINES FOR SUCCESSFUL MEASUREMENT

Productivity measurement occurs within a dynamic and complex organization. This means that the organization's culture, the values and experience of all the role incumbents within the organization, and the political context and the organization's history, will all bear on how the researcher or manager is perceived and the success of the effort. In short, some of these complex factors will help the measurement process and others will hinder it. All the researcher or manager has to figure out is which factors are which—which will make for success, and which are barriers. It is toward this very practical goal of making productivity measurement work that we direct this chapter.

Productivity Measurement Must Be Handled as a Change Strategy in the Organization

Change strategies require carefully thought out systems and approaches if they have any chance of success. Strategies for change require carefully laid-out groundwork. All expected barriers to the change must be acknowledged and considered at the earliest stages of the change. Because change in organizations is painfully slow, it is important to avoid the trap of using a technique to demonstrate productivity improvement early on. This "technique a month" trap will produce a short-term productivity success, if that. Employees become suspicious of the latest technique and usually decide that if they "stonewall" long enough, the new technique will go away. The productivity manager is also doomed to finding a new technique of the month, each one a little more clever than the last.

As with any change strategy those introducing productivity measurement and improvement processes can expect resistance from some people in the organization. It is important to identify those people who are the adaptors and innovators in the organization. They should be brought into the process early and often. For those who resist change, it is important that they be informed at all points in the process and brought into the effort, if possible, early on in the planning stages. Seek their opinions and feedback, but recognize that they may not embrace the process until there is critical mass in the organization that sweeps them into the change whether they want to or not (Tichy and Devanna 1986).

Create a Vision for Productivity Improvement Through Productivity Measurement: Expect to Provide Strong Leadership

Recent management studies tell us that the most effective managers are those who lead their units, organizations, and people (Bennis and Nanus 1985). One of the keys to effective leadership is creating a vision of the possibilities. It requires a belief in, and the dedication to, an idea or process that adds value to the organization and to the people in it. It requires a can-do attitude in the face of skepticism and barriers. It is, however, what makes successful organizations what they are today. The histories of IBM,

Hewlett-Packard, Apple, Ford, Sara Lee, Deluxe Check Printers, and Johnson and Johnson are characterized by visionaries who made things happen.

Productivity measurement in organizations requires the same kind of leadership. It is leadership that uses illustrations and images to help top management catch the vision. It talks, lives and breathes the possibilities of the process, in this case, productivity measurement. It is patient with top management, but also is able to point out the potential for solving strategic problems by looking at the productivity process as a powerful system for improving organizational health. In the final analysis, changing an organization so that productivity and quality are taken seriously requires a masterful selling process. When productivity measurement and improvement are seen as long term solutions to strategic effectiveness, top management can be brought on board to change rather easily.

The productivity manager has the equally challenging task of selling productivity measurement to all affected employee groups. Communicating the vision and possibilities is time consuming, requiring patience and perseverance. As has been noted, people embrace new ideas and procedures in different ways; some never do. One key to communicating the vision is to help find "win-win" examples in productivity measurement and improvement. Front line producers of goods and services are likely to read extra work, lost jobs, and harder work into the word "productivity." Rather, researchers and managers must identify and stress to individuals and the organization that the measurement system can bring pay-offs.

Involve and Get Buy-In
from Senior Management

The point of first attack in any organization that seriously wants to measure and improve productivity is senior management. We have already discussed the need to sell top management on the vision and possibilities. That alone is not sufficient to sustain productivity efforts. Senior management must do more than give their approval. They must be involved. Productivity efforts require massive changes in the culture, policies, and procedures of most companies. These changes will need more than the one-time approval of senior management, who then pass the responsibility on to a middle level manager. Senior management must be part of planning, communicating, organizing, and implementing all productivity measurement efforts.

This is not to say that productivity measurement and improvement are impossible without senior management support. Lacking such support, the process must begin as a small pilot, with little fanfare, for the purpose of finding a "champion." This usually gets the attention of senior management, and, hopefully, their support for broader efforts. This approach requires greater patience to accomplish productivity goals, often with fewer resources. Yet, the potential for productivity gains and contributions to organizational success over the long term is very real.

Aim Initial Efforts at Targets with a High Probability for Success

This guideline springs from two principles we have learned and relearned a number of times, and which seem to be true almost to the extent that they are nearly immutable "laws": (1) nothing succeeds like success, and (2) it's easier to get a win when a win is easy to get. The first principle attests to the fact that people not initially involved in a measurement effort are more likely to want to become involved if they see that it can work and might bring them success. The second principle states the obvious truth that the leader of a measurement effort will find it easier to make the measurement work where conditions for success (management support, a spirit of risk taking, energetic staff, and so forth) are already present.

Thus, our advice is that the researcher or manager who hopes to implement a productivity measurement procedure should first undertake a careful survey of the organization and seek out a high potential "win" situation. In our work, we have intentionally passed up an opportunity to tackle a truly major and significant productivity issue in favor of a less significant issue, simply because we wanted to start our work with a success. In such cases, we believe it is better to have tried and won, rather than to have never won at all.

Be Alert to, and Account for, the Political Ramifications of Measurement

The current distribution of power, and the continuing struggle to either maintain or acquire new power, is the process of politics in an organization. The current political milieu is based in part on the current organizational structure and procedures. Any change in procedures threatens some power bases, and offers others the opportunity for new power. The introduction of productivity measurement procedures into the current organizational context may be viewed (often rightfully so) as especially disruptive of the power balance.

The new measurement procedure may, for example, empower some employees to argue for more resources. Or, a manager who is used to making decisions based on information previously kept private may suddenly be confronted with having data bearing on decisions now more publicly available, and thus feels very threatened. The point here is that a new measurement procedure will inevitably either (a) gore someone's ox, or (b) be perceived as potentially goring someone's ox. In such cases, perception is acted on as reality, and the researcher or manager must act carefully to identify, account for, and ameliorate if possible, the immediate and potential political fallout from a measurement intervention.

**Grow the Productivity Measurement Effort
from the Ground Up**

This means that people in the grass roots levels in an organization are valued partners in productivity improvement efforts. They serve on the committees. They assist with and react to any productivity measurement plans. They must clearly agree that any output measures are those that they have control over. They must be given a hunger to know how productive they are. They must understand that they are the only ones who can really discover ways to make processes and work actions more productive (Moore 1987).

Productivity measurement systems imposed from above are likely to involve the traditional management-labor argument over who is responsible for productivity. When the process is a team effort, with multi-level personnel involvement, the process has real potential. Without it, we have witnessed work floor sabotage of the best measurement systems, where data is inaccurate or completely false, and interventions are agreed upon verbally but ignored in reality.

**Build On-Going Communication
Networks and Procedures**

One absolute rule in managing change is "no surprises." Because productivity improvement is a process in change management, the "no surprise" rule is critical.

An effective way to support ongoing communication is to involve personnel from all levels of the organization. One of their specific roles, in addition to participation in planning and implementation, is to communicate to their peers what is occurring in productivity improvement efforts. When peer networking is honest and open, skeptics may hold their skepticism, but have little fuel to feed their feelings.

Ongoing communication includes: posting results, updating newsletters, sending internal memos on progress and plans to all personnel, talking productivity in the workplace, and discussing the issue at the senior level whenever possible. Changing an organization requires extensive effort. Ongoing communication is the method to sustain vision and openness. It says "no surprises."

**Provide the Necessary Training and
Support to Implement and Sustain
Productivity Improvement Efforts**

The change we have discussed requires some new skills or at least the use of skills not often used in the workplace. It requires analytical skills to look at processes and see opportunities. It requires an ability to quantify and measure in simple ways. It demands interpretative skills so that gathered data can be put to good use. Productivity changes require the abilities to communicate, solve problems, and coach people concerning new processes.

Implementation often requires training in basic productivity and quality concepts. This training is especially critical at the producer level. Helping managers and supervisors prepare for change and leading organizational change is essential for success. Fundamental concepts in measurement must be taught to those who will be involved in first efforts. Helping team leaders and supervisors conduct productivity meetings is vital to productivity improvement.

These efforts need not be company wide, making the training task overwhelming. We have suggested that productivity measurement efforts might best begin with a pilot group or unit. The piloting of training efforts can occur simultaneously.

Some organizations may never initiate productivity measurement efforts, thinking that their workforce is incapable of mastering such sophisticated thinking and concepts. Our experience has shown just the opposite. In a manufacturing plant we worked with, high school educated parts painters were conducting experiments on the quality of paint applied to parts. They were experimenting with different thinner mixtures, heat controls, application processes, and part surface preparation. They could produce and interpret multi-variate data on the effect of each experiment and which process or combination produced the best quality paint job with the least costly inputs. When the data help job operators do their jobs better, they will readily learn what is needed.

Employees also need training in using data in decision making. People must be able to spot productivity trends. They must be able to take measurement data and decide what are the causes of both productivity gains and declines.

We have seen numerous organizations in the past five years commit significant resources to train people to measure productivity using "statistical process control" methodologies. The first need that is expressed in many of those same companies is, "we have all the data but we never make use of it." We have seen the best productivity charts, complete data on machine and people production, but blank faces when asked how that information is being used. Any productivity measurement system can fall prey to the same trap: Good data are available, but no one is using them.

The last significant training issue is supervisor and manager training in coaching and feedback skills. Because change produces a level of performer uncertainty, people will need to know very precisely when they have done things correctly and when they need to improve performance. Corrective feedback must be done in ways that protect the performer's self-esteem while making it clear that the performance is expected to improve. This is an art that many technically competent managers have not developed. They often have not received organizational support to develop the skill. When productivity measurement efforts are introduced, many performers will want to know if their performance meets expectations. Managers who catch their reports "doing things right" will find the right behaviors repeated. Early in the measurement process, positive feedback may make the difference between success and failure.

It is our belief that performers who are shown the concrete results of productivity and quality improvement efforts will take pride in their efforts. The best way to sustain momentum for this process is in building performer pride and the ownership of productivity measurement and improvement.

Evaluate the Productivity Measurement System and Diffuse the Process Across the Organization

The implementation of any productivity measurement system requires a backward glance as well as a plan for full implementation. Any system must be open for inspection and evaluation. In fact, those leading the process must be the leaders in evaluating the results. The only effective way to evaluate productivity measurement efforts is to have clearly defined goals and benchmarks. With those in place, productivity improvement efforts can be objectively evaluated. The goals of a 1% reduction in scrap rates, or a 2% increase in quality outputs, or a 1% reduction in material costs, while maintaining quality outputs, are all very measurable. Few will be able to argue with productivity results when such goals are achieved and important to organizational success (Guba and Lincoln 1981).

Evaluation provides the fuel for revising productivity measurement systems. Initial measures of outputs and inputs may need revision; evaluation will show where this is the case. Evaluation will feed directly into finding those areas where productivity can be improved. You have now gone full circle and are ready to implement additional productivity improvement efforts. Evaluation feeds the assessment process we mentioned earlier in the chapter.

Flexibility is essential for productivity measurement and improvement success. Organizations, people, and processes change. Each change may require a slightly different approach to what and how measurement is done. If the principles in this chapter are followed, it is not a "once done, home free" process. At the very point of success, adapting the process may be called for. With constant feedback from all personnel, fine tuning the process yields ever increasing productivity.

Evaluation of productivity measurement results must support a reward system for those responsible for the outcome. The organization must discover what the performers value in the way of a reward system. Some organizations can reward performers with public recognition, others must use financial means. The culture of the organization usually prescribes the type of reward. It is absolutely necessary that performers know that their contributions to increased productivity are noticed and rewarded. It is the single best way to sustain productivity and gain momentum. At the very least, all information about productivity progress must be made highly visible. We most often see charts and graphs of productivity growth in those companies that take productivity seriously (Cissell 1987).

After the initial pilot success in measuring and improving productivity, the next challenge is in diffusing the process throughout the organization. One of the best ways is to keep all personnel informed, using the same communications channels set up during the introduction phase of the project. Keeping internal curiosity high, but reporting the challenges and opportunities presented in the process, helps all employees, especially those not part of the pilot.

Keeping management informed on progress is vital for organization wide productivity efforts. Not only should management be involved in planning and implementing productivity improvement efforts, they should be actively involved in the evaluation and communication of results to their peers.

An especially effective method to implement this process organization wide is to use personnel from the pilot as mentors or coaches in other areas.

Their experience and success can be quite contagious. It also makes the system a peer-to-peer effort. Again, we would argue that this is very powerful because it is the producer-level performer who most knows where productivity gains are possible. Relying solely on management expertise may only slow the process of producer-level mentoring and hinder success in measuring and raising productivity.

SUMMARY

The reader with even a minimal level of experience in organizational intervention will recognize that these guidelines are relatively generic; this further attests to this chapter's opening statement that a productivity measurement effort is, above all, an effort to bring organizational change. Thus, our guidelines apply equally well to virtually any evaluation project or other organizational intervention.

Technical skills in measurement, data collection, analysis, and so forth, are clearly needed for successful productivity measurement. Researchers and managers hoping to implement productivity measurement procedures should clearly possess, or have access to, such skills. Equally important, however, and a note on which we wish to forcefully close this book, is that these researchers and managers must have an understanding of the organization in which they plan to work. How organizations function, the nature and context of politics and power, and the relationship of people to their organization are but some of the critical knowledge areas without which even the utmost in technical skill and knowledge are virtually useless.

The primary ingredient for success is, however, an energy and a commitment to do something to improve productivity. An honest, open project undertaken by a relatively unskilled practitioner, as long as he or she remains humbly ready to learn from mistakes and is willing to aim for small, incremental improvements, is as likely to be successful (if not more so) than a larger project staffed by the top productivity measurement consultants in the country. We hope that our little book is a catalytic ingredient in such an effort.

Virtually every organization needs to improve productivity and thus could benefit from measurement. And, virtually anyone can play the productivity measurement game with a good chance of success. What is needed is more players; more researchers, evaluators, and managers willing to begin to identify potential productivity improvement areas, willing to install measures to bring productivity issues into focus, and then willing to track the effects of productivity improvement interventions.

REFERENCES

Adam, E. E., J. C. Hershauer, and W. A. Ruch. 1981. *Productivity and Quality: Measurement as a Basis for Improvement.* Englewood Cliffs, NJ: Prentice-Hall.

Alkin, M., R. Dailak, and P. White. 1979. *Using Evaluations: Does Evaluation Make a Difference?* Beverly Hills, CA: Sage.

Ansari, A. and M. Ebrahimpour. 1988. "Measuring the Effectiveness of Quality Control Circles: A Goal Programming Approach" *International Journal of Operations & Production Management,* 8, 2: 59-68.

Baumol, W. J. and K. McLennan. 1985. *Productivity Growth and U.S. Competitiveness.* New York: Oxford Press.

Belcher, J. G., Jr. 1987. *Productivity Plus+.* Houston: Gulf Publishing.

Bennett, K. W. 1982, February. "Motorola Focus on Productivity & Quality is Worth a Look." *Iron Age,* pp. 61-64.

Bennis, W. and K. Namus. 1985. *Leaders.* New York: Harper & Row.

Blake, R. R. and J. S. Mouton. 1981. *Productivity: The Human Side.* New York: American Management Association.

Boileau, O. C. 1984, August. "Improving Quality and Productivity at General Dynamics." *Quality Progress,* pp. 16-20.

"Bottom-up management." 1985, June. *Inc.,* pp. 33-48.

Brinkerhoff, R. O., D. M. Brethower, T. Hluchyj, and J. R. Nowakowski. 1983. *Program Evaluation: A Practitioner's Guide for Trainers and Educators.* Boston: Kluwer-Nijhoff.

Buehler, V. M. and Y. K. Shetty. eds. 1981. *Productivity Improvement.* New York: American Management Association.

Campbell, D. T. and J. C. Stanley. 1966. *Experimental and Quasi-experimental Designs for Research.* Chicago: Rand McNally.

Chew, B. W. 1988, January/February. "No-nonsense Guide to Measuring Productivity. *Harvard Business Review,* p. 110.

Cissell, M. J. 1987, November/December. "Designing Effective Reward Systems." *Compensation & Benefits Review,* pp. 49-55.

Committee for Economic Development. 1983. *Productivity Policy: Key to the Nation's Economic Future.* Washington, DC: Author.

Cook, D. B. (1976, May). Automated Productivity Information—Necessity not Luxury. *Retail Control,* pp. 52-59.

"Corporate scoreboard." 1988, March 14. *Business Week,* pp. 122-127.

Deming, W. E. 1981. *Quality, Productivity and Competitive Positions.* Boston: MIT.

_____. 1983. *Out of Crisis.* Boston: MIT.

Gilbert, T. F. 1978. *Human Competence: Engineering Worthy Performance.* New York: McGraw-Hill.

Guba, E. G. and Y. S. Lincoln. 1981. *Effective Evaluation: Improving the Usefulness of Evaluation Results Through Responsive and Naturalistic Approaches.* San Francisco: Jossey-Bass.

Hamson, T. 1986, September. "Before Quality Circles—A Review of 'Productivity: A Practical Program for Improving Efficiency' by Claire F. Vough with Bernard Asbell." *Quality Circles Journal* 3: 44-50.

Hartman, A. C. and T. B. Towner. 1984. "Operations: Proper measurement: Key to productivity." *ABA Banking Journal* 76: 164-166.

Haskew, M. 1985. "IMPROSHARE and Quality Circles: Teamwork at John F. Kennedy Medical Center." *Quality Circles Journal,* 8: 24-26.

Hayes, G. E. 1985. *Quality & Productivity: The New Challenge.* Wheaton, IL: Hitchcock Publishing Company.

"Involved People Make the Difference in Manufacturing." 1982, February. *Modern Materials Handling*, pp. 17-20.

Japan Productivity Center. 1983. *Measuring Productivity.* New York: Unpublished manuscript.

Kay, C. R. 1986. "A University Approach to Participation: Quality Circles in Higher Education." *Quality Circles Journal*, 9: 14-17.

Kendrick, J. W. and D. Creamer. 1961. *Measuring Company Productivity: Handbook with Case Studies.* New York: National Industrial Conference Board.

Kendrick, J. W. and E. S. Grossman. 1980. *Productivity in the United States.* Baltimore: Johns Hopkins University Press.

Kohler, C. and S-W. Rainer. 1985. "Introducing New Manufacturing Technology: Manpower Problems and Policies." *Human Systems Management*, pp. 231-243.

Krogh, L. C. 1987, November/December. "Measuring and Improving Laboratory Productivity/Quality." *Research Management*, pp. 22-24.

Lachenmeyer, C. W. 1980. *Assessing Productivity in Hard-to-Measure Jobs.* Hempstead, NY: Hofstra University.

Landy, F., S. Zedeck, and J. Cleveland. eds. 1983. *Performance Measurement and Theory.* Hillsdale, NJ: Lawrence Erlbaum.

Lehrer, R. N. 1983. *White Collar Productivity.* New York: McGraw Hill.

Lenk, Gerry. 1988, June. "Quality." *Supervision*, pp. 11-13.

Measuring Productivity. 1983. Tokoyo: International Productivity Symposium.

Megalli, B. and G. Sanderson. 1978, November/December. "Productivity—Quality of Working Life a Key Factor?" *Labour Gazette*, pp. 500-504.

Miller, D. M. 1984, May/June. "Profitability-Productivity Price Recovery." *Harvard Business Review*, p. 145.

Moore, C. W. 1987. *Group Techniques for Idea Building.* Newbury Park, CA: Sage.

National Center for Productivity and Quality of Working Life. (1983). *Improving Productivity Through Industry and Company Measurement.* Washington, DC: Author.

Nollen, S. 1979, September/October. "Does Flexitime Improve Productivity?" *Harvard Business Review*, p. 12.

Perry, N. J. 1988, December 19. "Here Come Richer, Riskier Pay Plans." *Fortune*, pp. 50-58.

Puckett, A. E. 1985, September/October. "People Are the Key to Better Productivity." *Industrial Management*, pp. 12-15.

Ranney, G. B. 1986, Spring. "Deming and the 14 Points: A Personal View." *Survey of Business*, pp. 13-15.

Riggs, J. L. and G. H. Felix. 1983. *Productivity by Objectives.* Englewood Cliffs, NJ: Prentice-Hall.

Rummler, G. A. 1976. "The Performance Audit." In *Training and Development Handbook*, 2nd ed., edited by R. L. Craig. New York: McGraw-Hill.

————. 1982a, October. "Linking Training to Organization Performance." (Available from: The Rummler Group, 25 Franklin Place, Summit, NJ 07901).

————. 1982b, October. "Organizations as Systems." (Available from: The Rummler Group, 25 Franklin Place, Summit, NJ 07901).

Ryan, J. 1983, December. "The Productivity/Quality Connection-Plugging in at Westinghouse Electric." *Quality Progress*, pp. 26-29.

Sherman, G. 1984-1985, Winter. "Japanese management: Separating Fact from Fiction." *National Productivity Review*, pp. 75-79.

Shetty, Y. K. 1986, Spring. "Quality, Productivity, and Profit Performance: Learning from Research and Practice." *National Productivity Review,* pp. 166-173.

Shetty, Y. K. and V. M. Buehler. eds. 1985. *Productivity and Quality Through People.* Westport, CT: Quorum Books.

Simers, D., J. Priest, and J. Gary. 1989, January. "Just-in-Time Techniques in Process Manufacturing Reduced Lead Time, Cost; Raise Productivity, Quality." *Industrial Engineering,* pp. 19-23.

Taylor, F. 1947. *Scientific Management.* New York: Harper.

Tichy, N. M. and M. A. Devanna. 1986. *The Transformational Leader.* New York: John Wiley.

Thomas, B. W. and M. H. Olson. 1988. "Gain sharing: The Design Guarantees Success." *Personnel Journal* pp. 67-72.

Turner, L. 1989. January. "Three Plants, Three Futures." *Technology Review,* pp. 19-23.

Tyler, R. 1983. "Rationale for Program Evaluation." In *Evaluation Models,* edited by G. Madaus and D. L. Stufflebeam. Boston: Kluwer-Nijhoff.

Widtfeldt, J. R. 1982, January. "How IEs can Contribute to, Gain from a Quality Circle." *Industrial Engineering,* pp. 64-68.

Wilson, J. D. 1983, December. "Logic . . . not Magic: A Comprehensive Quality Program Improves the Product and Reduces Costs." *Quality,* pp. 60-61.

Wright, N. H., Jr. 1982, February. "Productivity/QWL-Part 2." *Management World,* pp. 17-20.

Yamaki, N. 1984, Autumn. "Productivity: Japanese Style—Part 2—Small Group Activities in Mitsubishi Electric Corporation—A Case Study." *Management Japan,* pp. 10-18.

Yamamoto, S. 1985/1986, Fall-Winter. "Tradition and Management." *International Studies of Management & Organization* pp. 69-88.

ABOUT THE AUTHORS

Robert O. Brinkerhoff began his training and evaluation career in 1964 as an officer in the U.S. Navy, in charge of a number of curriculum design and training projects. He completed a doctorate in program evaluation at the University of Virginia in 1974. Brinkerhoff has provided evaluation and management consultation to a number of major corporations and agencies in the United States, Australia, Portugal, and South Africa. He is the author of six books and several articles and chapters on training and evaluation. Brinkerhoff is currently Professor of Leadership at Western Michigan University in Kalamazoo.

Dennis E. Dressler began his human performance improvement career in 1969 as an educator and leader in non-profit agencies. His education includes a master's degree in supervision and instruction, and graduate work in human resource development. Dressler has consulted with Fortune 500 companies in pharmaceuticals, automotive production, and banking. He is the author of articles on organizational effectiveness, training, and values clarification. Dressler is currently an Account Executive at Training Strategies, Inc., Kalamazoo, MI.